Sufism and Modern Science

Dr. Mehmet Bayrakdar was born in 1952 in the village of Bayavşar in the Beyşehir district of Konya. After graduating from the Faculty of Theology, Ankara University in 1973, he went to Sorbonne University (Paris) for his doctorate. In 1979, he joined the Chair of Islamic Philosophy at Ankara University Faculty of Theology and became a professor in 1991.

He worked in many universities in Turkey and other countries. Between 2000 and 2007, he was a member of the Higher Council of Religious Affairs. He is currently a lecturer at Faculty of Arts and Sciences, Department of Philosophy, Yeditepe University. He knows Arabic, French, English, Persian, Latin, Spanish, Italian, Malay, Classical Greek and Japanese. He has a number of books to his credit.

BOOKS BY MEHMET BAYRAKDAR

1. *Du Coeur à Toi*, Paris, 1979.
2. *History of Science and Technology in Islam*, TDV Publications, Ankara, 1985; (2nd Edition: Rehber Publications, Ankara, 1992).
3. *Introduction to Islamic Philosophy*, Ankara University Islamic Studies Faculty Publications, Ankara, 1985; (2nd Edition: TDV Publications, Ankara, 1987).
4. *Evolutionist Creation Theory in Islam*, Insan Publications, Istanbul, 1987; (2nd Edition: İslamiyat Publications, Ankara, 2002).
5. *Phenomenology of Islam Worship*, Akçağ Publications, Ankara, 1987.
6. *Dawud al-Qaysari*, Ministry of Culture and Tourism Publications, Ankara, 1989.
7. Sufism and Modern Science, Seha Publications, Istanbul, 1989.
8. *La Philosophie Mystique chez Dawud de Kayseri*, Ministry of Culture Publications, Ankara, 1990.
9. *Yunus Emre and the Philosophy of Love*, Türkiye İş Bankası Publications, Ankara, 1991.
10. *Idris Bitlisi*, Ministry of Culture Publications, Ankara, 1991.
11. *Islam and Ecology*, DİB Publications, Ankara, 1992.
12. *Freedom of Expression in Islam*, Turkish Democracy Foundation, Ankara, 1995.
13. *On the Book of Islamic Truth*, Fecr Publications, Ankara 1995.
14. *Introduction to Philosophy of Religion*, Fecr Publications, Ankara, 1997.
15. *History of Islamic Thought*, Anadolu University Open Education Faculty Publications, Eskişehir, 1999.

Sufism and Modern Science

Prof. Dr MEHMET BAYRAKDAR
Translated by Dr Mohsin Ali

STERLING PUBLISHERS (P) LTD.
Regd. Office: A1/256 Safdarjung Enclave, New Delhi-110029.
Cin: U22110DL1964PTC211907
Phone: +91 82877 98380/ +91 120-6251823
e-mail: mail@sterlingpublishers.in
www.sterlingpublishers.in

Sufism and Modern Science
Dr Mehmet Bayrakdar
Mahcubiyet Oybiileri Ersin Yilmaz
© 2021, Dargah Yayinlari
Translated by Dr Mohsin Ali
Edited by Sanjiv Sarin
ISBN 978 81 950824 3 8

All rights are reserved.
No part of this publication may be reproduced, stored in a retrieval system or transmitted, in any form or by any means, mechanical, photocopying, recording or otherwise, without prior written permission of the original publisher.

Printed in India

Printed and Published by Sterling Publishers Pvt. Ltd.,
Plot No. 13, Ecotech-III, Greater Noida - 201306,
Uttar Pradesh, India

Contents

Preface to the New Edition   viii
Preface   ix
*Introduction: Interpretations of Sufism and
   Modern Sciences*   x

1. Sufism and the Scientific Method   1

Self or Ego (Nafs)   15
  1. Nafs al-Ammara (The Inciting Self)   17
  2. Nafs al-Lawwama
     (The Self-Accusing Self)   17
  3. Nafs al-Mulhamah (The Inspired Self)   18
  4. Nafs al-Mutma'inna
     (The Self at Peace)   18
  5. Nafs al-Raziyyah (The Pleased Self)   19
  6. Nafs al-Marziyyah (The Pleasing Self)   19
  7. Nafs al-Kamil
     (The Perfect or Pure Self)   19

2. Sufis as Scientists   23

Chemist Sufis   25
  1. Ja'far al-Sadiq   25
  2. Jabir ibn Hayyan   25
  3. Dhul-Nun al-Misri   29
  4. Shaheen Al Khalwati   29

Astronomer Sufis	30
1. Abd al-Rahman al-Sufi	30
2. Al-Ghazali	31
3. İbrahim Hakkı Erzurumi	32
Physician Sufis	34
1. Qutb al-Din al-Shirazi	34
2. Akshemseddin	34
Technician Sufis	37
Ahmed Süreyya Emin Bey	37

3. Modern Scientific Views in Sufism — 44

Panbioism	44
1. Panbioism and Sufis	44
a) Cosmic Worship	*47*
b) Cosmic Dance and Movement	*48*
c) Eschatological Evidence	*48*
d) Existential (Ontological) Evidence	*48*
e) Experiential Evidence	*49*
2. Panbioism and Modern Science	50
3. Panbioism and Similar Philosophical Views	51
4. Panbioism and Panpsychism	51
5. Panbioism, Animism and Vitalism	53
6. Panbioism and Hylozoism	53
Converting One Element into Another or Converting Copper into Gold	54
A New Creation at Every Moment or the Cosmic Dance	58

The Multi-Universe Idea	62
The Possibility of Overcoming Time and Space/Relativity and Destructibility of Time and Space	66
The Divine Light of Prophet Mohammad and Energy	70
Eye of the Heart or Sinoatrial Node	71
Organic Information Theory and Human Embryological Development	74
The Sufi Whirling or Sema Ceremony and the Structure of the Universe and the Atom	78
1. Sema Ceremony, the First Creation and the Last Creation	79
2. Sema Ceremony, the Structure of the Universe and the Atom	79
Conclusion	*82*
Bibliography	*84*
Index	*88*
Translator's Note	*95*

Preface to the New Edition

The first edition of this book was published in 1988. I suppose the publisher made a few more prints later. People used to ask me about the book from time to time when it was out of stock. I thought it would be useful to republish the book with some minor additions.

On this occasion, I found it necessary to refer to an important point here. There is a wrong conclusion which some readers infer from the book. They get the impression that Sufism or Islamic mysticism makes a person a scientist or scholar in the context of natural science. There is no such thing in consideration here. The main purpose of this book is to show that Sufism gives depth or profoundness of thought and intellect to scholars who have, for example, studied medicine or chemistry, and who have also become Sufis by some means at the same time.

Sufism is basically a spiritual psychology and the art of inner education. In this sense, as long as its principles are followed, Sufism can keep a person away from the unnecessary and temporary things of the world and give the person depth of mind and consciousness in the field of research. This, in turn, may lead to some breakthroughs and discoveries in the fields of science that the mystic is interested in. Sufism neither makes someone a scientist who only deals with mysticism nor does it make one do scientific discoveries.

I would like to thank the editor Erhan Güngör and other officials and employees of Insan Publications who contributed to this new edition of the book.

22 August 2016

Prof. Dr Mehmet Bayrakdar
Yeditepe University

Preface

I have been doing research on the Philosophy of Science and the History of Science for a long time now. These researches showed me that many views in Sufism, especially on creation, the universe and the physical and spiritual structures of humans, are very close to and parallel with today's data of modern science and the modern theories.

Here, in this grand book called *Sufism and Modern Science*, I want to show the closeness between Sufism and science in a short but concise and understandable language. I hope it can be useful.

Effort is from us; guidance is from Allah.

Associate Prof. Dr Mehmet BAYRAKDAR
Ankara, 21 September 1988

INTRODUCTION
INTERPRETATIONS OF SUFISM AND MODERN SCIENCES

The term modern science is used to express the science of our age. Of course, this implies that the science of our age is different from the sciences of ancient times. This difference is explained as the difference in subject, method and the understanding of science. However, there are differences of opinion on this issue between philosophers and historians of science.

With the advent of the inept positivists in the 19th century who did not know about the rich human history, a fashion called "modernity" entered the picture. Of course, with the amount of knowledge flowing from history, there are some new things emerging in our age that did not exist earlier, but this does not mean that the old is worthless or primitive. What will be the name of our era in the 40th century? Each era will have its own innovations compared to the earlier ones, and this is quite natural. Could we rename the theory that we still use in geometry, known as "Pythagoras Theorem", as Chinese theory since it was recorded in the primitive language around 1000 BCE, roughly 650 years before Pythagoras? Could we call the knowledge of astronomy that Babylonians, who lived in 2000 BCE, and could precisely calculate and determine the solar and lunar eclipses beforehand, as primitive? Isn't there something ideological in the 19th century Westerners' representation of the ancients as primitive? To put it more clearly, is it not a false, ideological trick or delusion that some 19th century and later period cultural historians have put forward certain theories to glorify the West, where scientific research have increased in number with time, and to establish the creativity of the Western mind and therefore the superiority and domination of the Western race, as if it were a miracle, without having a past?

Many Western science and cultural historians, along with many other thinkers, testify that the belief of a number of their colleagues that the birth of modern science happened with positivism is something that is delusional and unreal. For example, while Ritchie Calder, a science historian and ideologist, states the beginning of so-called modern science with Francis Bacon (1561–1626). A thinker and a scientist, who both grew up in the early New Age, that is, the Renaissance, Daniel E. Gershenson and Daniel A. Greenberg, also assert that modern science started with Anaxagoras (500–428 bce), one of the ancient Greek thinkers, in their book *Anaxagoras and the Birth of Scientific Method*. Especially when it comes to astronomy, there are those in the West who claim that modern science started with Copernicus (d. 1543). For example, Thomas S. Kuhn says so in his book *The Copernican Revolution*.

If modern science is to be given such an arbitrary start, Muslim scientists are more worthy of it than Westerners. Because, on the one hand, the Westerners, who were credited for the birth of modern science, themselves say that they were inspired by the Muslim scientists. And even if they do not say so, historically there is a lot of evidence to prove it. On the other hand, there are several Westerners who have called Muslims "modern". For example, Cardano (d. 1576), the esteemed scientist and thinker of the Middle Ages, considers the great Muslim scientist and thinker Al-Kindi (796–866) as the founder of psychophysics and one of the 12 greatest personalities of the world, while the astronomer Levi ben Gerson (d. 1344) mentions the great Muslim scientist Al-Bitruji (d. 1217) as the founder of modern astronomy in his book *Wards of the Lord*.

The important point in terms of the history of science is to acknowledge the contribution of all humanity in today's science. When 5,000 years ago people of Ur calculated the solar year to be 365 days, 6 hours, 15 minutes and 41 seconds, their calculation was just a little off with an extra of 26 minutes and 55 seconds. Do we need to deny the contribution of the people of Ur, who made such a modern calculation, in the history of science? Again, after seeing that the contents of a chart, found in Til al-Harmel near today's Baghdad and written exactly 2,000 years before Euclid's theorems of geometry, match perfectly the contents of Euclid's *Elements of Geometry*, should the contribution of these people be disregarded in the history of science?

The claims of the historians of science, who deny and ignore these facts, and the committed ideologists who are brainwashed by the positivist movement, are as follows: for something to be a science, it must be observed, put in the laboratory and be the subject of an experiment, and be expressed through scientific methods such as deduction or induction. This understanding emerged only in the positivist age. There was no such understanding in the metaphysical and primitive ages before that. While we will discuss the criticism of this understanding in chapter 1, we want to give some facts here.

Didn't the "ancient" and "primitive" people resort to observation, experimentation or other methods while presenting their scientific views? Weren't what we call modern scientific methods present in the ancient times? Of course, they were. For example, Anaxagoras succeeded in the production of water clocks after long experiments in front of the public. The chemist Jabir ibn Hayyan, who was a Sufi, had a laboratory in which he did chemical experiments and observations in the place called Damascus Gate of Baghdad, remnants of which can be found today. We learn from the archaeological excavations that the ancient Egyptians and Babylonians made numerous observations and did experiments in agriculture, botany, animal husbandry and astronomy in even earlier times. History clearly records that Abu Bakr al-Razi (865–925) was became blind during chemical experiments.

The definition of a scientist should also be taken in a broader sense. If science is defined as revealing accurate or nearly accurate information about nature and human structure, or facts that are generally accepted throughout history, or applicable knowledge, then the person who comes up with this knowledge should be considered a scientist, regardless of their profession and disposition. For example, will we not consider Mendel, whose education and profession was religion, but as a result of his researches on plant and animal genes gave the law that is accepted as correct even today and is known by his name, i.e., Mendel's Law, a scientist? Of course, we will.

Now, we would like to switch to Sufism along with the above example. Did the Sufis, as generally considered, occupy themselves only with just moral and religious matters? When the works of Sufis are read carefully, we find that most Sufis were very interested in the structure of nature, the essence and reasons of natural phenomena, and the biological and spiritual structures of human beings.

Since the Sufis often expressed their views symbolically and not in more concrete terms as a requirement of the language of philosophy of the period, what they said could not always be clearly understood. However, when compared with today's sciences, we find the principles and roots of many scientific facts in their sayings. Regardless of the different methods of communication between scientists and Sufis (we will talk about this again in chapter 1), we see that the results of their findings reveal the truths that are accepted today as being scientifically correct.

The following question may arise here: Did the Sufis (at least some of them) not make any visible, tangible scientific inventions in spite of all their scientific theories? Why did they not put the scientific knowledge they discovered into practice?

Converting a scientific theory into an application is called applied science or technique. There are innumerable scientific theories and hypotheses which have not been applied to any practical use. This does not mean that they are not absolutely correct, nor does it mean that they are wrong in any way. All theories are still considered scientific, despite consensus or controversy over them. At the same time, today's scientific understanding is different from a positivist's earlier understanding of scientificity. The strict and even unrealistic rules of positivism do not determine scientificity any more. The subject of science has expanded so much due to its structure and subject that it is not possible for every scientific theory to enter the laboratory and to express it with exact mathematical formulas. Moreover, many theories that were expressed mathematically in the past have become debatable today and are considered far from being scientific.

Returning to the main issue, the answer to the above question, for a scientific theory to turn into a technical one, there should be a dire need of it first of all and secondly, the necessary tools and equipment must be found in advance for this. Thirdly, it must be the technician by training, who brings forth the scientific thesis; and fourthly, the nature and subject of scientific theory must be appropriate for technical application or practice.

As we will see, first of all, most of the scientific theories put forward by Sufis are not subject to technique in terms of their structure and subject, since they concern cosmology and creation. Sufis are not people who deal with technique because their education and training is different. The history of science also shows us that it is not always the person who puts forward the theory who brings it into practice, but it is people who come afterwards Some of the Sufis, such as Jabir ibn Hayyan, who were both chemists and Sufis, tried to put their scientific theories into practice. As we shall see, some of the Sufis, just like many chemists, accepted the theory that one element could be transformed into another by humans. As a result, they tried to obtain gold from silver, copper and other metals and minerals. Among these Sufis, Dhul-Nun al-Misri and Jabir ibn Hayyan are the most well-known. This theoretical knowledge only became practical for the first time in the 20th century, when Rutherford converted nitrogen to hydrogen. This led to the construction of the hydrogen bomb. We will come back to this issue later.

1

SUFISM AND THE SCIENTIFIC METHOD

What is method? What do scientists understand by scientific method? First, we want to get into the subject with these questions.

Especially after the Renaissance and Reform movements, the Western world started to progress slowly in science and the Islamic world started to decline. As a result of this, Western science began to become independent of the Islamic scientific tradition. At the same time, science began to prevail over Christianity, which had excluded scientific inventions and theories from the very beginning. This advance of science began to change the worldview of individuals, especially Western philosophers and scientists. Thus, inevitably, the understanding of science and scientific method started to change in parallel with these. Finally, the Age of Enlightenment [1685–1815] came. This period was considered as the beginning of free thought in the history of Western thought. This era had two main features: The first was the attempt to use materialist philosophical movements against the church as a means of practical proof as well as the ideologization of these philosophies in line with the world view. The Age of Enlightenment, with these characteristics, soon transformed into was called the positivist era. With positivism, the change in the understanding of science and scientific method reached its final point.

To the positivists, according to A. Comte, who was the founder of positivism in the first place, science was nothing more than the answer to the question of how physical things are visible. Science had started to deal with not the questions of why and what for, but only with the question of how. Such an understanding of science, whose subject and purpose had thus been narrowed, of course, resulted in an understanding of method or methodology as its goal.

First, the so-called principles of reason and logic would be reconsidered and evaluated; humans would not go beyond them. So the mind would get struck by itself. For example, some of them were: sameness, contradiction, the absence of the third state.

Later, methods such as experiment, deduction and induction, which we call the methods of obtaining science, would be re-determined, and these would be regarded as unchangeable and absolute. Scientific data was always expected from all this. It would be postulated that if the mind operated only within these rules, everything was rational and scientific; if human approached events only with these methods, the result was scientific. Otherwise, there could be no talk of science and scientificity.

As we have stated before, both the rules that we call the "rules of reason" and all the methods prescribed by the positivists, were encountered in every period of ancient human history of science. The experimental method in particular, is represented as if it had begun with positivism, but that is not the case. Abu Bakr al-Razi, who made chemistry experiments, had his eyes blinded by smells and gases that emanated from chemical compounds and chemical analysis. We know that Jabir ibn Hayyan, who lived before him, had a laboratory, the ruins of which were found in Damascus Gate of Baghdad. One cannot even count the number of the astronomical observations made in those times. Al-Biruni and Al-Khazini determined the specific gravity and density of objects through experiments, Ibn al-Haytham discovered the dark room (camera obscura) and did experiments – his experiential and experimental scientific studies are some of the other known facts. There are many more examples.

Thus, the only thing that changed with the Enlightenment and positivism was the view of science and scientific methods. There is rigidity and inflexibility in the nature of this view. Is this view itself scientific? Or is it just an assumption and delusion? Couldn't the mind of a person who keeps his field of thought wide go beyond the rules that are called principles of reason?

When we look at the history of sicence and when we examine the great scientific discoveries and theories, we understand that positivists like A. Comte and the old and new positivists who think like him, are not at completely correct. We realize that their views are nothing more than just speculative assumptions. How?

Consider the law we call "Archimedes Principle" and the manner in which Archimedes discovered it. Did Archimedes find the law of buoyancy with a scientific method in the sense that positivists or those with that mentality explained science to be? No!

To find this law, it was enough for Archimedes to be a thinking person. He was someone who was always preoccupied in his mind, thinking all the time about the secrets of the universe. He was not someone who would just pass by events around him – rather he thought about them. He thought about how and why these events took place. It was at such a moment that he entered the bathhouse to bathe. While taking bath, when he saw that the water bowl did not sink into the pool upon falling into it, his mind immediately evoked an association and established connection to the ongoing thought in his mind. He couldn't help crying out loud, "I found it, I've found it!" Surely, many people had seen that a plank or a bowl thrown into the water floated without sinking, but they just saw the action. They could not do anything beyond seeing. For Archimedes, to find the Law of Buoyancy, it was enough for him to be a thinking person – a person who really thinks. He never made any methods, plans or programmes in advance to find the Law of Buoyancy.

Almost all the fundamental discoveries of science emerged like Archimedes's discovery. The situations of all the other explorers were like Archimedes. They found their discoveries in situations that were not actually coincidences, but can be called accidental – unscheduled, method-less. In fact, many times they approached the things they wanted to find, know and explain with different methods, but their discoveries took place about something quite different from what they were looking for. They achieved their goals as a result of some associations.

For example, take Newton. He was a person of science who thought and used his mind like Archimedes. He would not just look at things happening around him, he would think. He sat at the foot of an apple tree lost in his thoughts, perhaps to ease his tiredness. Soon a ripe apple fell on his head. Here, the falling of the apple on his head proved to be enough for Newton to find the Law of Gravity. Hadn't everyone seen an apple, a pear or a stone fall earlier? Of course, millions had. But they did not analyse it like Newton as they were not thinking about it.

Do you know how Edison, who is remembered with gratitude by everyone though some people even debated whether he would go to Heaven or Hell, found the electric bulb?

Edison wanted to transform electrical energy into light, illuminating everything. He kept on doing experiments for days, months and years without a break. He kept saying to himself that if he did this then the result would be that and if he did that then the result would be this. But after all this, nothing happened except for exhaustion and botheration. But he continued to think.

One day, again lost in his thoughts, he continued to work at the table after having dinner with his children and wife in the living room of his house. The children were also playing around and making noise. A sentence of his wife that she uttered after the seeing room's situation so that the children did not disturb their father and interfered in his work, became enough for Edison to be a source of inspiration. His wife said to the children, "Quiet, you empty-headed lot!" Upon hearing these words, Edison started thinking about it and said to himself, "Empty, huh! Let me do the experiment in a vacuum." He did his experiment in a vacuum and what did he see? Light! Thus, the word "empty" that his wife spoke was a source of inspiration for Edison. The incredible electric bulb and its light that we see is the work of an "empty" phrase, an "empty-headed" phrase.

There is a proverb in Turkish, "What I hoped for, what I found." You have heard of the famous Röntgen. One day he set out looking for something, hoping for something. But what he found was not what he was looking or hoping for. Finally, when Röntgen saw the X-rays, he said, "What I hoped for, what I found." Röntgen set out to work on Maxwell's electromagnetic theory, which was still controversial in his time. He began by repeating Sir William Crookes's experiment and used his tube. (As is known, in order to experiment on his theory called "The Fourth State of Matter", Sir William Crookes used a tube shaped like an airship formed by the space created between a cathode forming a negative pole at its narrow end and a cross metal anode forming a positive pole at its broad end.) He tried to examine the state of the fourth kind of particles that Crookes had postulated. He repeated his experiments many times. In one of these, he detected light waves on the fluorescent salt and saw a red ember. When he wanted to put a piece of cardboard painted in black and see the result, he observed that all the light suddenly disappeared. On 8 November 1895, he conducted a similar experiment and saw again that a warm, ember-like light was formed in the dark room on the salt he had placed twenty feet away from the tube. These lights would now be called Röntgen rays. Later, when Sir James Mackenzie asked him what he felt when he observed the incident, he said, "The thought that I hadn't thought." Because Röntgen was investigating the electromagnetic phenomenon, it was not his intention to find the X-rays.

The same is true for Dalton, who introduced the modern atomic theory. He also found what he did not expect. Dalton was actually a meteorologist, not a chemist. He also found the structure of atoms while investigating how water was absorbed by the atmosphere.

Some of the thinking minds have come to a scientific conclusion about an event just by continuously thinking about it. Then, if either the same person or someone else could find the opportunity to research and experiment it, that thought became science. For example, Sir Oliver Lodge, in 1900, simply thought that the Sun emitted radio waves. Until 1931, this remained a thought. That year, Bell used very sophisticated radios in telephone laboratory to study changes in atmospheric phenomena. K.G. Jansky heard violent rustling when the antenna was pointed in a particular direction. Lodge thought that some stars and the Milky Way were emitting radio waves. Like Röntgen, he found things other than what he was looking for. Later, J.S. Hey confirmed, with a more advanced technique, that the Sun emitted radio waves.

There are many more such examples. Many of the inventions and discoveries came about by chance. Few scientific inventions or discoveries have been made with the so-called scientific method and techniques. The most suitable of such methods are the methods of experience and observation, which, as we have said before, are not the methods of the recent period as positivists claimed, but the methods used since ancient times. But even with these methods, if there is no leap in thought, no association, no stimulus, it is not possible to discover or invent anything.

So, there is neither an understanding of reason nor the scientific method prescribed by people who are not actually scientists, but who are brokers in the name of science. If they were actually scientists, wouldn't we have today a lot of scientific discoveries and theories from August Comte and his friends, the representative of the positive mind? Unfortunately, no scientific invention or discovery has been passed on to us from him and those who think like him. What we have from them is just empty promises and a lot of literature in the name of science.

In fact, if this kind of proposition is studied carefully, it will turn out to be against science. Because if science is something that can only be observed, can be the subject of experimentation, put into a laboratory, can be repeated with the same reasons and results whenever desired, and can be mathematically expressed, there will be innumerable scientific theories and thoughts that cannot fit into these measures but are accepted as true.

Consider, for example, the theory of evolution. How do you express this mathematically? How will you be able to put it in the lab and experiment? How will you observe? In any case, the formulation of the theory of evolution does not allow this by the virtue of its very definition. Because, according to Darwin, evolution takes place in such a long time that it is impossible for hundreds of people, let alone one person, to notice or observe this in their lives. So either evolution is not a science, or the understanding of science of positivist and strict rationalists is not scientific.

It has now been understood well that science and thought are not just the "voice of reason", as Cartesian philosophy said and later positivist philosophy repeated. In the formation of science and thought, the mindset and mentality of the scientist are as important as the psychology, sociology and history of the person. The fields of sociology and psychology of knowledge draw our attention to this point. Knowledge and science are not just a dry, mind business. The psychological structure, social behaviour and social factors play a great role in the formation of knowledge and science. The historical environment in which a person grows up, or the accumulation of culture until it reaches the person, and the scientific heritage and development in history are as important as intelligence. If it were not for the historical development of scientificity, the mind of today's modern persons would be no different from the mind of the persons considered primitive. Until recently, many people who asserted that the history of philosophy must be known in order to practise philosophy said that it was not necessary to know the history of science to practise science. But now it is understood that knowledge of the history of science is necessary and useful in order to practise science. This has become an important point of departure for those who practise philosophy of science.

So, from what we have said so far, it follows that just one particular method is not necessary or compulsory for science. Humans can obtain results from science in different ways in different situations. There is only one condition for all this. It is enough for the person to be a thinker, for him or her to use their brains to understand whatever is happening around them, and even go to sleep thinking of the problems to be solved. It is possible to make the most profound scientific discoveries even in sleep. Everything is method for the thinking person.

At this point, this is what the famous philosopher of science Paul K. Feyerabend says in his work *Against Method:*

> The idea of the method that leads to the work of science, which is absolutely fastened, which contains unchangeable and rigid rules, is confronted with the results of historical research. So we cannot find a single rule that has not been violated from time to time, although it may be reasonable and absolutely accepted in epistemology (science or theory of knowledge). It is true that such violations are not accidental events. They are not the consequences of lack of information or carelessness that should be avoided. On the contrary, we understand that they are necessary for progress. Indeed, one of the most striking characters of the recent discussions on the philosopher [philosophy] of science and the history of science is that it has been understood that some thinkers put forward the events and developments like the emergence of atomism in antiquity, the Copernican revolution, the birth of modern atomism (kinetic theory, dispersion theory, stereochemistry, quantum theory), and the gradual emergence of light wave theory, either because they did not attach themselves to "known" methodological rules or because they unwittingly demolished those rules.[1]

---

1. Paul K. Feyerabend, *Against Method, Outline of an Anarchistic Theory of Knowledge*, p. 23.

Feyerabend's slogan "Anything goes", which means that any method is permissible in scientific methodology, is also famous.

Considering the history of science, it is impossible not acknowledge that Feyerabend was correct. Many philosophical currents pushed Feyerabend to this conclusion, not only examining and evaluating the history of scientific discoveries and inventions but also bringing new interpretations of the method and source of science and philosophical thought that emerged in the early twentieth century. Let's take a brief look at these.

At the beginning of our century [i.e., 20th century], there were positivists and those who were against the rigid understanding of science and methodology of those who thought like them. The leading ones were the mathematician and philosopher Edmund Husserl and the philosopher Henri Bergson. The thought of not believing and not trusting a pure mind can be traced back to Kant in the modern age. Kant's famous quote can teach us a sufficient lesson on this subject: "When I think with pure reason, I do not believe in science, it is not possible to explain science; but I still have knowledge." Undoubtedly, Kant wanted to point out that science and knowledge are not the products of pure reason. Even before Kant, Descartes and his students, who started to deify the mind, did not find the mind sufficient in some subjects. They resorted to intuition. However, the subjects they applied to intuition were not in the field of science, but rather in the field of metaphysics. They said that knowing God and the self is not possible with the mind, but only through intuition.

We know the general philosophy of the Jewish-born German philosopher and mathematician Edmund Husserl (1859–1938) as phenomenology. What is the significance of this philosophy for our topic?

Before Husserl, Hegel (1770–1831) described phenomenology as the experiential science of consciousness, but did not make a distinction between consciousness and objects regarded consciousness and objects as one, and sought the truth within the whole of the data of consciousness, which he called absolute knowledge. Whereas Husserl consciously sought real knowledge, not in the data of consciousness, but in the whole "lived intuition" that consciousness acquired through wilfulness or intention leaping into the essence of objects, considering that objects cannot be counted as a consciousness. In his view, intuitionism and the deep experience of objects should have been preferred to the crude rationalism and empirical sophism of the ancients in explaining the facts of things. Husserl did not accept knowledge as the reduction of things to self or in the name of self by mind and senses. He considered mind and senses to be a form of subjectivism that is far from reality. Only objective knowledge could be obtained by establishing an intuitive link between two such irreducible realities, leaving the self as self and objects as themselves, without reducing objects to the self.

A similar intuitive philosophy was advocated by the anachronistic French philosopher Henri Bergson (1859–1941). Intuition plays the biggest role in Henri Bergson's philosophy as well. According to him also, the real knowledge of metaphysical beings as well as the real knowledge of physical things could only be obtained with the help of intuition.

The intuitive philosophies of Husserl and Bergson were not only philosophical, they changed the West's understanding of science and scientific methodology. They began to be applied to the different fields of science and methodologies. Thus, the hegemony of crude positivism gradually began to disappear. For this reason, many mathematicians such as

Georges Bouligand in his work *Les aspects intuitifs de la Mathématique*, and Elie Cartan and Brouwer in their various writings began to argue that even the most rational science – mathematics – is an intuitive science. They argued that real mathematics was only based on intuitive data. Likewise, it has been argued that even the science of logic itself, which is the most logical science, is intuitive. The thinker A. Heyting [1898–1980] was the leading name among these logicists. He proved that the principle of non-contradiction of the third state in logic is not logical and it is valid under certain conditions only.

On the other hand, as we have said earlier, when a person, i.e., a thinking person, goes to sleep with a thought in the mind, they can have a scientific observation in their dream. Even a dream is a method. Let's make some brief explanations on this subject.

Inspired by the information given in the Quran and Hadith about this topic, it was argued centuries ago by many Islamic thinkers, especially Al-Ghazali, that dreams– real dreams – are a source and a method of knowledge, especially in metaphysical matters. For example, S. Freud, who studied the dream phenomenon in psychology and psychoanalysis, first denied the acquisition of information through dreams, but later, especially in his work *Le rêve et son interprétation*, argued that information can also be obtained through dreams.[2] Later, some scientists put forward similar theses on this subject. Before discussing the views of some of these modern people, let's summarize briefly what is the mechanism of this work according to Al-Ghazali.

How humans can obtain knowledge through dreams is briefly described in Al-Ghazali's work titled *The Revival of the Religious Sciences (Ihya Ihya' Ulum al-Din)* as follows:

---

2. S. Freud, *Le rêve et son interprétation*, French translation by H. Legros, p. 134.

Some of the people who can cleanse their soul through Sufism (sometimes there are moments when the human soul is cleansed by itself, so in those moments some of the normal people too) can obtain knowledge in sleep. Because, while sleeping, the soul becomes more active by getting rid of the pressure of the body and can contact the self by rising to the *Lawh al-Mahfuz* (The Preserved Tablet), where all the sciences are engraved; so it can reflect information from there to the heart. As a result of this reflection, the human heart can obtain some information through sleep while dreaming. However, this information is often not self-evident and cannot be clearly understood, as it comes with symbols. The dream needs to be well interpreted.[3]

We come across a similar statement in the *Marifetname* (Book of Gnosis) of İbrahim Hakkı Erzurumi.[4]

Morton Schatzman, an English author and thinker, known for his work on dreams and sleep, says that dreams are not only a method of obtaining information on metaphysical matters, but information on every subject. In his article in the *New Scientist* magazine, he advises readers to think about different complex issues before going to sleep.

It should not come to you as strange that dreams are considered a scientific method because there are several examples where they have provided scientific information. For example, Friedrich August Kekulé, the famous German chemist, dreamed about the structure of the benzene molecule. Unable to solve the structure of this molecule with several scientific experiments and methods, the chemist went to bed one night when his mind was occupied with this subject and saw six snakes in his dream, one biting the other's tail. When

---

3. Al-Ghazali, *Ihya*, Volume IV, p. 436, 456, 459; See also Volume III, p. 25.
4. M. Bayrakdar, "Learning about the World and Post-Death Events by Dreaming According to İbrahim Hakkı Erzurumi", *National Education and Culture*, Issue 25, 1984, pp. 26–31.

he woke up in the morning, he interpreted his dream and realized that the structure of the molecule in question was hexagonal.

As we have seen, we should not regard the dream as a simple event. We think that the conclusion that should come out of what we have told so far has already been understood. But let's repeat again: the understanding of science and scientific method is by no means crude and dry rationality and logical positivism. No one has ever made a scientific discovery with deduction and induction or other rules of reason and logic. Anything from rational thinking to dreaming, from observation of external emotions to intuition can be a scientific method. Indeed, science is the work of all of them.

In such a case, the talk now necessarily comes to Sufism or Islamic mysticism. What is Sufism or Islamic mysticism? In general, it is a method with the main purpose to obtain accurate information about Allah and is nothing more than a methodology. Sufism is a means and method for humans to approach Allah and at the same time it is the knowledge of this method. There is a point to remember here: as we briefly pointed out in the introduction, although the main purpose of Sufism is to approach Allah and to know about Allah through deep experience, it is undoubtedly seen by many Sufis as a method of understanding the facts and secrets of nature. Particularly, Imam Al-Ghazali gave a wide coverage to the study of nature and natural events and some movements such as following Wahadat al-Wujud (Unity of Existence) and Mevlevism, which are among the later Sufism movements. However, as a requirement of Sufism, the fields of physics and metaphysics, spirit and matter, visible and invisible are intertwined without distinction from each other, and the results are displayed from a theological aspect, in other words, in terms of the existence and agency of God, the ultimate goal of everything. It can be seen clearly and distinctly that the physical knowledge of nature is mentioned in all of this.

Now let's see what kind of a method and methodology Sufism is in general, without going into too much detail and not depending on any particular Sufism school of thought. Then, we will briefly make some observations about the types and characteristics of mystical knowledge obtained after learning about this method.

As it is known, one of the reasons for the birth of Sufism is that knowledge is not just a matter of reason, as opposed to theology and philosophy, both of which defend that knowledge is only reason, logic and sensation. On the contrary, Sufism believes that it is a matter of intuition, deep understanding and perception, and the centre of these is not the mind, but the heart and the soul. In order for a person to acquire knowledge with these centres, he or she must go through some psychological stages of evolution, which is generally referred as "training of the self or ego (nafs)" in Sufism. That is, it is the cleansing of one's soul and, in this manner, the rise towards perfection.

Self or Ego (Nafs)

What is the self or ego (nafs)? How is it cleaned?

It is quite difficult to express the exact meaning of the word self or ego (nafs) as used in Sufism. The word has been used so much in Sufi works and such a wide-ranging meaning has been attributed to it that it sometimes even includes other Sufi idioms such as the soul, body and personality. However, it can be said that the self or ego (nafs) is the pure human self, which is the source of many positive and negative emotions and instinctive powers, including the mind, and which is connected to the body in one aspect and to the soul in the other. Since the self or ego (nafs) is both the object and the subject of knowledge, the self or ego (nafs) itself must be known and recognized. This is the basis of Sufism. A person can only know other beings, including Allah, if he or she knows their own self well. For this reason, the Hadith, "Who knows their soul, knows their Lord" has been made famous by the Sufis.

According to Sufis, the only condition for a person to know their own self or their existence, and then other beings, is to educate and train the self or ego (nafs), transcend the feeling and mind, and reach the sources and means of information that we can generally call intuition. Disciplining or educating the self or ego is the dulling of some negative and non-essential desires of the human self-attached to the body or channelling them in a good direction. In this process, the desires and forces related to the soul will be strengthened and, consequently, the dominance of the soul on the self instead of the body will be established. There are a number of physical, biological and psychological rules for accomplishing this, which vary according to each Sufi school of thought, but essentially achieve the same result. The individual will reach a certain discipline of the self or ego by following these rules and will also rise to the optimum level by going through the different levels of training of the self or ego with these rules.

There are several stages in the process of the absolution of the self or ego, the number of which varies according to different Sufis. Generally, these are the following as mentioned in the Quran:

1. Nafs al-Ammara (Surah Yusuf, 53)
2. Nafs al-Lawwama (Surah Al-Qiyamah, 2)
3. Nafs al-Mulhamah (Surah Ash-Shams, 8-9)
4. Nafs al-Mutma'inna (Surah Al-Fajr, 27)

5. Nafs al-Raziyyah (Surah Al-Fajr, 28)
6. Nafs al-Marziyyah (Surah Al-Fajr, 28)
7. Nafs al-Kamil

Each of these stages of the self has its own characteristics. The means of each of them to obtain knowledge and the attribute and nature of the knowledge obtained are also different. Let us briefly see these stages of the self.

1. Nafs al-Ammara (The Inciting Self)

This stage is where the pure human self that has not been cleansed or educated at all, governs the human being. Lust and all kinds of bad and empty attributes are peculiarities of this self. It lacks real knowledge and it is content with the data of the sensory organs. At this stage, human beings are almost no different from animals. For this reason, Sufis call a person of this stage an animal person. At this stage, the individual thinks that the Shari'ah corresponds to its external or apparent meaning only.

In order to get out of this stage and rise to the next stage, one should follow a middle path in eating and drinking, sleep less, not speak too much unnecessarily, pay attention to his or her moral behaviour and keep reciting "La ilaha illa Allah" (There is no God but Allah). If a person does these things constantly, he or she will cleanse their soul a little.

2. Nafs al-Lawwama (The Self-Accusing Self)

This is the stage in which a person begins to become conscious of their own self. It is the stage where the self starts accounting for itself, rejoice for its good deeds and begins to condemn itself for its bad deeds. The individual begins to realize their bad deeds and regret them.

At this stage, the individual stops being contented with just conforming to the apparent or external meaning of the

Shari'ah, begins to submit to their inner self, that is, their soul and turns towards nature. The subject and scope of their knowledge expands a little more. At this stage, the person does not only think and perceive the visible realm with the mind and senses, but also begins to think of the invisible realms, especially the stage of existence called the Barzakh Realm, with the eyes of their heart. Knowledge is at the degree of ilm-ul-yaqeen (the knowledge of certainty). This is a stage where the person starts their spiritual cleansing gradually. The person keeps reciting the word, "Allah, Allah" at this stage. Eating less, drinking less, sleeping less, doing good deeds are the characteristics of a person in this stage. Love and affection are dominant in the individual in this stage. Also, the person can sometimes see some truths through dreams at this stage.

3. Nafs al-Mulhamah (The Inspired Self)

This is the stage where the bad attributes of the human self are completely abandoned and the good is separated from the bad. In this stage the person conforms to both the apparent and inner meanings of the commandments and prohibitions of religion. It is in this stage that one passes to the realm of the soul. It is no longer the self or ego that directs the person, but the soul. The different moods of love are dominant over the person in this stage. The subject of knowledge is both nature and the Realm of the Angels. Knowledge is at the level of ayn-ul-yaqeen (the vision of certainty). The chanting and remembrance is "Hu" (a name of God) at this stage.

4. Nafs al-Mutma'inna (The Self at Peace)

This is the assured stage where the self or ego is cleansed and purified. The self has now reached the Realm of Magnificence. Its knowledge is the absolute wisdom. Knowledge is at the degree of haqq-ul-yaqeen (the final level of certainty gained through experience). The remembrance and chanting is "Al-Haqq, Al-Haqq" (one of the names of Allah). In this stage the person gradually takes some inspiration and makes some discoveries.

5. Nafs al-Raziyyah (The Pleased Self)

This is the stage in which the self accepts itself and is satisfied with its good deeds and cleanliness. The person is now the representative of Allah at this stage. He or she becomes the recipient of the manifestation of the deeds, names and attributes of Allah. "Al-Hayy, Al-Hayy" is the remembrance and chanting in this stage. Knowledge is manifestations [of Allah] now. Whatever name or attribute of Allah that is manifested in the heart of the person, true knowledge is given to him or her as required by that particular attribute and name. The person roams in the Realm of the Divine.

6. Nafs al-Marziyyah (The Pleasing Self)

Here the self has been so much cleansed and everything human and physical has been discarded in such a manner that Allah has become pleased with that self. It is the stage where the individual gains Allah's consent. The person has no will of their own as he or she is surrendered to the will of Allah, along with everything of theirs. The individual watches the Realm of the Unseen in this stage and learns about the things at the level of the truth. The remembrance and chanting of this stage is "Al-Qayyum, Al-Qayyum".

7. Nafs al-Kamil (The Perfect or Pure Self)

This is the highest and the last of the stage of the self or ego. In this stage, the person has perfected himself or herself in every way. They are one with Allah now; whatever they do, they do it under the will of Allah. Whatever they hold, they hold it with the hand of Allah; whatever they hear, they hear it with the ear of Allah; and whatever they see, they see it with the eyes of Allah. The realm of the Unseen and the State of Testimony is the realm of the perfect human at this stage. Whatever the individual knows from these realms, they know them as truths. Their knowledge is the absolute truth. Their knowledge is no longer restricted to time and space. They can know and anticipate things in advance.

A person who passes all these stages, cleanses their self or ego, surrenders themselves to Allah and puts their trust in Allah, does not only obtain knowledge about God, they can also obtain knowledge about events they want to know about, or Allah can give the knowledge directly to this person's heart. There are several types of knowledge that can be obtained as a result of the cleansing of the self. The diversity of these depends on the rank and degree of the cleansing of the self.

The names of this knowledge are as follows: wisdom, discovery, revelation, inspiration, manifestation and conquest.

Wisdom and discovery: The common features of these are the knowledge that a person obtains through their own effort, through the heart, as a result of the cleansing of their own self or ego. Wisdom refers to the real knowledge about Allah, and discovery refers to the type of true knowledge about the natural events.

A person who has cleansed himself or herself of the pressure and desires of the body increases the connection of the self to the soul and gives up to the will of the soul. The soul also can obtain knowledge from the realm of the Lawh al-Mahfuz (The Preserved Tablet), to which it is attached, as the knowledge of all the things that are and will be in the universe are engraved in the Lawh al-Mahfuz. So the person discovers by reflecting these engravings on their heart.

Revelation (hads): Revelation means intuition and refers to the knowledge obtained in this way. It is the general description for different types of knowledge such as inspiration, manifestation and conquest. These are the knowledge that Allah puts into the heart of the person, according to the stage he or she is in, without their effort or intent, after they reach a certain level of cleansing of the self. The subject matter of these types of knowledge can be varied. It can be knowledge of the future and past human events, as well as knowledge about all kinds of natural events.

As can be understood from what we have said so far, Sufism is actually nothing more than a method and a methodology. The effort to achieve even stronger forces of heart and make the soul the source of knowledge by cleansing the self or ego with practice and mental activities, freeing it of bad deeds and thoughts and passions of the body, and overcoming the external emotions and mental forces, is the preparation of the individual for obtaining knowledge.

Lastly, let us recall the words of the great scientist and philosopher Ibn Sina, in terms of showing how deep contemplation, inner cleanliness and prayer help science and the field of science and how it is a method of concentration:

> Not being able to solve the issue of the middle term in syllogism, when the problems of logic continued to shake me, I continued to attend the mosque constantly and humbly worshiped and prayed to the Creator of all things until He revealed the secret of these matters to me and made the difficult easy.[5]

Among the Sufis, those who deal with the philosophy of nature and those who research the secrets of nature have pioneered many correct views about natural phenomena long ago that modern science has just started talking about

---

5. Ibn Sina ve Jurjani, *Sîretü'ş-Şeyhi'r-Râîs*, English translation by W.E. Gohlman, *The Life of Ibn Sina*, Arabic text p. 28, English text p. 29.

today, with knowledge such as wisdom and discovery, as well as inspiration and manifestation. However, most of their views were either symbolically expressed or were ahead of their times and they were abandoned either because they could not be comprehended or considered as mischief and quackery. By examining some of the views which the Sufis evaluated in these ways and comparing them with the data of the modern sciences they are related to, we will try to show in later chapters of this book that those views were not conjuring tricks, and today they have gained scientificity with modern science.

2

SUFIS AS SCIENTISTS

If we talk of Sufis today, different people say different things about them, each interpreting from their point of view. According to some, they are charlatans, perverts and even faithless persons. Some see them as fanatics, rude, illiterate dervish, withdrawn from the world, and even a reactionary. According to some, they are true Muslims who have devoted themselves to asceticism and piety (taqwa), and who live a religious and moral life. Regardless of these views of the Sufis, there are many Sufis beyond all these descriptions. In terms of their way of life and thoughts, they are neither charlatans, nor atheists, nor sluggards who have completely withdrawn themselves from the world. They are those who embrace both religion and the world, without separating them from each another. They deal with world affairs and natural sciences as well as religious sciences. For this reason, many Sufis were and are also scientists at the same time.

When we look at the branches of science that scientist Sufis generally dealt with in the past, we see that these are the fields of chemistry and alchemy, astronomy and astrology, and even medical sciences. The reason for this is that Sufis want to know everything along with its outer appearance, its manifestation, its inside, its essence and its inner reality. In particular, it stems from their desire to learn the metaphysical knowledge of beings rather than only their physical knowledge. The outer appearance of the universe appearing to the eye and the ear is not important, its secret and confidentiality appearing to the Eye of the Heart are essential. In other words, the quantitative and descriptive knowledge of the being provided by physics and mathematics is not important, but the qualitative knowledge given by metaphysics is necessary. Sciences such as chemistry and alchemy, astronomy and astrology, and medicine, have attracted more attention from Sufis, as they are the closest branches to metaphysics and, like metaphysics, lead humans to the metaphysical knowledge of existence.

Sufis paid great importance especially to chemistry and astronomy. It can even be said that chemistry, excluding people like Abu Bakr al-Razi [who was mainly a physician and scientist by profession], is a science completely developed by Sufis in the history of Islamic science. Almost all Muslim chemists, from the early ones such as Ja'far al-Sadiq and Jabir ibn Hayyan to the chemists of the last period such as Omer Shifai and Ali Bey İzniki, were Sufis.

Let us look at some Sufis who were mystic scientists and who became famous in these sciences.

Chemist Sufis

Many Sufis specialized in the field of chemistry and chemical science.

1. Ja'far al-Sadiq (d. 739)

Ja'far al-Sadiq, who was the founder of the Ja'fari or Imamia sect and considered the sixth of the Shiite imams, was a person who dealt with many branches of knowledge, including Sufism and chemistry. He can be regarded as the second chemist in Islam after Khalid ibn Yazid (d. 708). Although some 20th century writers say that Ja'far al-Sadiq did not deal with science, it has been proved otherwise from the research of Julius Ruska, a historian of science, and from the fact that the famous chemist Jabir ibn Hayyan considered him as his teacher for all the branches of knowledge.[6]

2. Jabir ibn Hayyan (721–815)

Jabir ibn Hayyan, who is considered one of the greatest chemists of Islam and the medieval period and the second in rank among the Sufi chemists, was known as 'Geber' by Westerners due to his great influence on Western chemistry. Geber is the Latinized form of Jabir. Chemistry and alchemy studies in the West began with the translation of his works into Latin and other local languages.

Jabir ibn Hayyan, also known as 'Sufi', was interested in mathematics and astronomy, besides chemistry. He wrote commentaries on Euclid's *Elements of Geometry* and the *Almagest* of Ptolemy. He was interested in the philosophies of Socrates, Plato and Aristotle. He also has a work on logic and philosophies one on poetry.

Jabir ibn Hayyan attracted attention especially with his

studies on chemistry. He was not only interested in theoretical chemistry, but did chemical experiments too. While living in the city of Kufa, he had his own laboratory in its suburb nearby known as the "Damascus Gate".[7]

Jabir ibn Hayyan wrote several books of chemistry, many of which were translated into Latin, gave great contributions to today's chemistry science and the chemical industry. His mercury–sulphur based theory of the formation of metals had been accepted as an unchangeable theory all over the world until the 18th century, which is considered to be the beginning of modern chemistry. Among the more important contributions of Jabir ibn Hayyan is that he first discovered citric and nitric acids and prepared sulphuric acid for the first time. Among his contributions that helped in the development of the science of chemistry after him is his even more important view that the sciences, especially chemistry, must be based on experiment and experience. Before Jabir ibn Hayyan, chemistry was a complete speculation and a semi-magic, and called alchemy. As a result of his understanding of science, alchemy gradually gained the identity of a true science. This understanding of his is seen in his following words, which are an advice to chemists, and are so modern as if they came from the mouth of a modern scientist:

> The first fundamental in chemistry is that you do practical research and experimentation. Because anyone who does not perform practical research and does not do experiments can never reach even the lowest degree of competence in scholarship. You, son! Do experiments so that you may gain knowledge.
>
> Scientists are not delighted with the abundance of tools and materials; they only enjoy the perfection of their experiential methods.

---

7. E.J. Holmyard, *Makers of Chemistry*, Oxford, p. 54.

A representative drawing of Jabir ibn Hayyan drawn in Medieval Europe
(A. Chelazzi, Florence)

Jabir's distillation furnace
(Drawing by E.J. Holmyard)

Jabir ibn Hayyan, together with the other famous Muslim chemist Abu Bakr Zakariya al-Razi (865–925), dominated the history of the world of chemistry for nearly a thousand years after his death. Two great schools of chemistry, "Followers of Jabir" and "Followers of al-Razi", were formed in the East and the West. Today, there are more than three thousand chemistry books in Arabic and Latin as well as in Mongolian attributed to Jabir ibn Hayyan. Although some of those books are certainly his own, many of them were written in his name by his Eastern and Western students who were brought up in the School of Chemistry of the Followers of Jabir ibn Hayyan.[8] In the 19th century Western writers had a misconception that Jabir was not a real personality, but a mythical one. This stemmed from the fact that the School of Chemistry of the Followers of Jabir ibn Hayyan influenced the people of the Middle Ages so much that many legends grew about him which simply did not fit the contents of books of science. He became the subject of Western folk tales and fables.

A page of one of Jabir's Arabic chemistry books
(Bodleian Library, MS. Marsh, 70)

---

8. E.J. Holmyard, 'Introduction' in *Works of Geber*, Translated by Robert Russell.

3. Dhul-Nun al-Misri (d. 859)

Another famous Sufi chemist included in the School of Chemistry of the Followers of Jabir ibn Hayyan is Dhul-Nun al-Misri. Al-Mısri, who was also knowledgeable about new Platonism, was famous as a philosopher, a chemist, and especially, a Sufi. In Sufism, he is seen as the first person to distinguish between "Spiritual states (Hal)" and "Stations (Maqaam)". Apart from a few, almost none of his works on chemistry and alchemy have been traced, so it is impossible to say what all new information he talked about in these books.[9] We only know the names of these books. Famous ones among these are *Ruknu Ahbar*, *Sikah* and *Kitabu'l-Aca'ib*.[10]

4. Shaheen Al Khalwati

Another example of a Sufi chemist is Shaheen Al-Khalwati. He was one of the followers of Dede Ömer Ruşeni, who took the Khalwati sect to Egypt and North Africa just before 1500. This Khalwati sheikh, who was probably from the Azeri Turks if not from the Anatolian Turks, was the most famous mystic of his time in Egypt. He had many students. The sheikh had a deep interest in chemistry and alchemy. As An-Nablusi reports, the sheikh had got so much involved in chemical experiments that his students, who had come to learn about Sufism from him, and his followers, abandoned him and attached themselves with another Khalwati sheikh Şemseddin Muhammed Demirtaş.[11] But unfortunately, we do not have much information about Shaheen al-Khalwati's chemistry research today.

---

9. For Dhul-Nun al-Misri's view of the science of chemistry and alchemy and some remaining pieces, see M. Berthelot *La Chimie au Moyen Age*, Vol. 2.
10. Ibn-Nedim, al-Fihrist, Neşr, G. Flugel, Leipzig, 1871–72, p. 355, 358; Brockelmann (C), GAL. Vol. I p. 199, 521.
11. Tevfik al-Tavîl, at-Tasavvuf fi Misr ibbân al-Asr al-Osmânî, quoted from the work of Abdü'l-Ganî an-Nablusi called *ar-Rihla*, Cairo, 1946, p. 78.

Astronomer Sufis

Astronomy was a popular science for many Sufis.

1. Abd al-Rahman al-Sufi (903–986)

The most famous astronomer Sufi was the great astronomer and Sufi Abd al-Rahman al-Sufi. Drawing attention with his personal observations and investigations, Al-Sufi is famous for his works on stationary stars. His work, *Book of Fixed Stars* (*kitāb suwar al-kawākib*), which includes these studies and is a catalogue of fixed stars, is one of the three masterpieces in this field –the other two belong to Ibn Yunus and Uluğ Bey.

Sagittarius Constellation by Abdurrahman al-Sufi

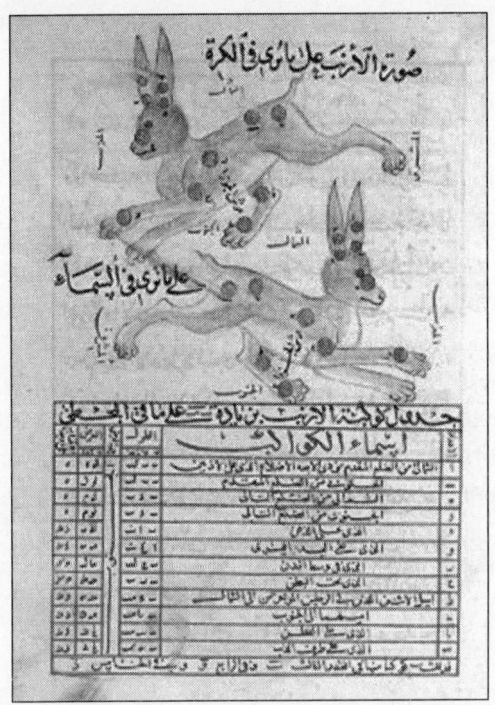

The Lepus (mountain hare) constellation by Abd al-Rahman al-Sufi

Although there is a similarity between this catalogue of fixed stars of Abd al-Rahman al-Sufi and that of the famous Argelander, which was written later, the former has a more scientific and original value. Abd al-Rahman al-Sufi determined and evaluated the places of some astronomical constants before anyone else. Abd al-Rahman al-Sufi, had also studied very long-term variations of the luminousness or éclat of the stars in his catalogue.

2. Al-Ghazali (1055–1111)

The famous philosopher Al-Ghazali was also an astronomer Sufi. In fact, Al-Ghazali was never trained as a Sufi or an astronomer if we take into account his upbringing and education. Al-Ghazali, who became famous as a scholar of religious sciences, became interested in philosophy and

Sufism at the height of his fame and educated himself in these sciences also to the degree of being famous for them as well. His interest in astronomy started with his interest in philosophy, which was considered one of the mental and philosophical sciences at that time.

We see that especially in his philosophical works, Al-Ghazali was interested in the philosophy of nature. He was also particularly interested in astronomy. We understand this from both his use of astronomical information in his work named *The Incoherence of the Philosophers (tahafut al-falsifah)*, which he wrote in order to refute the ideas of philosophers about the seniority of the world, and from a work on astronomy. The Arabic version of the latter is not available, but a Latin translation is preserved in the Bodleian Library in Oxford. Unfortunately, we do not know much about the content of this work as it has not been published yet. The work is named *Tractatus de Planets*.[12]

3. İbrahim Hakkı Erzurumi (1703-1780)

Another astronomer Sufi was the Turkish thinker İbrahim Hakkı. Although like other scientist Sufis, he too dealt with many fields of sciences, he was more famous as an astronomer and a Sufi.

Since special studies of Ibrahim Hakkı's views on positive science in general and in the field of astronomy in particular have not been conducted, we do not know for sure whether he contributed to science with his original ideas. Just by looking at the section on astronomy in his book *Marifetname (Book of Gnosis)*, it cannot be said that he introduced innovations in this field. He only summarized the views of the ancients. Despite this, we can view İbrahim Hakkı as an important figure, especially in terms of our history of science. He tried to revive the positive science

12. Oxford, Erfurt 8°, 79, 14c.

in the Islamic world, which had been abandoned years ago, especially in Ottoman Turkey. Even if he contributed no innovations, this effort itself is remarkable given the times he lived in.

Besides *Marifetname*, İbrahim Hakkı also discussed the science of astronomy in his work *Rubbü'l-Müceyyeb*. He talked about the use of an astronomy tool called "Jayib Board". The instrument is used to determine the time and meridians of its location. His work *Menâzil-i Kamer* is in Turkish with 180 couplets. It talks about the days, months, seasons and the states of the moon. Another of his works is called *Hey'etü'l-Islam*. This work in Arabic generally provides information about Islamic astronomy.

Physician Sufis

There were many Sufis who were famous as physicians.

1. Qutb al-Din al-Shirazi (1236–1311)

One of the few scientists belonging to the Islamic world in the 13th century was Qutb al-Din al-Shirazi. His father [Zia' al-Din Mas'ud bin Mosleh Kazeruni (d. 1250)] was a physician Sufi. Following the path of his father, he became interested in medicine and Sufism at a very early age and specialized in these sciences. Later he also dealt with other positive sciences, especially physics, mathematics and astronomy. For this purpose, he went to study at the famous Maraga Madrasa and its observatory. There he took lessons from Nasir al-Din al-Tusi and other teachers. However, he became famous as a doctor and Sufi during his lifetime. He came to Anatolia and took lessons from Sadr al-Din al-Qunawi about the mystical movement of Wahdat al-Wujud (Oneness of Being or Unity of Existence).

Al-Shirazi, who was a member of the Ibn Sina School in medical science, produced pioneering works in this and other branches of science. He wrote an important commentary titled *Sharh Kulliyat'l-Qanun* on Ibn Sina's work *The Canon of Medicine* (*Qanun fi al-tibb*).

2. Akshemseddin (1390–1459)

One of the typical examples of physician Sufis was the famous Turkish scholar known as Akshemseddin. His real name was Shemseddin Mehmed bin Hamza. He learnt religious sciences first, then he learnt about medicine and Sufism as well. He was especially famous for his talents in medicine and Sufism. For this reason, he was given the nickname

"Second Lokman Hekim (physician)" along with the titles of "Doctor of the Souls" and "Doctor of the Bodies".

Akshemseddin, one of the disciples of Haji Bayram Veli and one of the scholars during the Conquest of Istanbul period, wrote some important works on medicine and Sufism. Among the ones known to us are *Risalat an-Nuriya*, *Khall-e Mushkilat* and *Maidat ul-Hayat*. Many people wrongly refer to his last work as *Maddat ul-Hayat*.

Akshemseddin's notable contribution to both Turkish and world medical science was the discovery, for the first time, of the microbe and the hereditary nature of some diseases. He explained this in his work named *Maidat ul-Hayat*:

> All diseases have their origin and seeds according to their genetic types as in plants and animals, like the seed and root of grass. Diseases such as gaucher disease, leprosy and gout that are passed down from father and mother through inheritance can reappear even after seven years. The seeds of diseases caused by food and drink germinate and grow quickly.[13]

It is clear from this that Akshemseddin was the first scholar who talked about the microbe about four-and-a-half centuries before Louis Pasteur (1822–1895). Akshemseddin also talked about the causes of some diseases being hereditary for the first time, at least a century before Girolamo Fracastorius (1478–1553). The interesting thing is that Pasteur, like Akshemseddin, used French words for the microbe, which correspond to the words "seed" and "root" in Turkish. However, unlike Pasteur, Akshemseddin could not prove his discovery experimentally, since the microscope had not been invented yet and the science of microbiology had not come into the scene yet.

---

13. Akshemseddin, *Maidat ul-Hayat*, Fatih, Millet Library. Ali Emiri, Medicine 126, V. 50.

So far, we have briefly mentioned about some Sufi scientists. Many of these Sufis had been trained in these sciences from the beginning. Some of them became interested and engaged in these sciences at some later stages of their lives. That is why their scientific views and thoughts, which we will discuss ahead, are neither the product of their speculative and imaginary endeavours nor poetic fantasies. These are the products of their research and produced by these Sufis with skills and efforts equal to those of scientists of that age, by giving importance to intuition as a method in science. The source of their scientific theories and opinions, which are better understood today, was their research as scientists for some and for others it was their intuitive powers.

But here it would be appropriate to state the following as well: since the understanding of science and scientific knowledge has differed from time to time like everything else, a thought and a view considered as science in one era could be seen as a dream without reality in the next era. Or, on the contrary, a mental effort that has been regarded as purely a fantasy in earlier periods of time can become a science that can be proven, experimented and experienced in the later periods of time. For this reason, some of the Sufis' thoughts, especially about cosmology, were often seen as mere dreams in the earlier times, since the understanding of science at that time was not sufficiently developed. These thoughts were not somethings that fitted into the scientific logic of those times. For example, it was not possible to think of turning copper or any other similar metal, into gold. Similarly, no one could understand then if somebody said that living and non-living things had a soul, a memory and a living life. Stating that the atom could break was regarded as poetry only. The claim that there were worlds and galaxies other than our world in the universe would remain empty words that did not even need to be thought about. But these and similar "dreams" of Sufis appear as new discoveries today. In the next chapter, we will discuss some similar views on this.

Technician Sufis

There were important Sufis who were also trained in technical and mechanical fields.

Ahmed Süreyya Emin Bey

We also come across Sufis who were interested in technical and mechanical matters in the history of Islamic science. The best-known example of these is the Ottoman technician Ahmed Süreyya Emin Bey. Before talking about his important invention, let's introduce him briefly.

Ahmed Süreyya Emin Bey was born in Istanbul in 1848 and died in therein April 1923 at the age of 75. He was buried in his family cemetery next to Yahya Efendi Mosque in Ortaköy, Istanbul. His father was Emin Bey, the chief clerk in the imperial court who studied in the palace school of Ottomans. His grandfather was Haji Ibrahim Agha, who was in the service of Mihrişah Valide Sultan. Ahmed Süreyya Emin Bey completed his primary, secondary and high school education in Istanbul. He was a member of the Post and Telegraph Ministry Board of Directors for a while, but then resigned from this duty of his own will. He married Hatice Atiyetullah Hanımefendi and two sons were born from this marriage.

Ahmed Süreyya Emin Bey was raised within the Qadiri tariqa (Sufi order) since his youth and was the fourth Pir-e-Sani of the order. There is a Divan (collection) of his poems.[14] Ahmed Süreyya Emin Bey is famous for inventing the first Rapid Shot Field Cannon in the world in 1868. Ahmed Süreyya Emin Bey started his work in 1866 when he was 19 and finished it in 1868, when he turned 21, that is, within two years.

---
14. This divan was published under the name of *Divan-e Süreyya* by M. A. Özkardeş in Istanbul in 1960. Its second edition was published in 1998.

As is known, the Ottoman Empire was producing war material in Tophane-i Amire (imperial armoury) and Tersane (ship-building yard). As a result of the financial crises in the Ottoman Empire and the developments in the war industry in Europe, these institutions had lost their utility in the 19th century. Most material had started to be procured from abroad. However, the Ottomans continued to develop new technology and products. They attempted to start a smoke-free gunpowder factory. A new military factory was opened in Zeytinburnu with the initiatives of Cin Izzet Pasha. Some weapons, such as field guns, were cast and made there. This factory attracted the attention of Ahmed Süreyya Emin Bey. In fact, Ahmed Süreyya Emin Bey, who was not in military service, made all the plans and drawings of the Serial Firing Field Cannon himself, after getting a work permit to work there. The cannon was also capable of being disassembled and transported. He spent 500 gold coins from his own pocket and gave the cannon to Sultan Abdülhamid II as a gift. This cannon brought great prestige to the Ottoman Empire.

Thus, Ahmed Süreyya Emin Bey achieved a great success as the first person in the world to prove that rapid-fire cannon could be made. This success also shows that Ahmed Süreyya Emin Bey had an understanding far ahead of his times. He heard about the official announcement made by the French Government, which called on technical persons and engineers to investigate the problem of gas coming out of the touch-hole while the cannon was fired, which reduced the speed and power of the cannonballs. He solved this problem with one of his inventions while working on his ongoing projects. He designed a cover of the gunpowder chamber which prevented gas leaks from the breech by closing the touch-hole with a firing device and also designed two types of gas rings, one for steel and the other for bronze cannonballs.

Ahmed Süreyya Emin Bey

Ahmed Süreyya Emin Bey also conveyed this new invention in a petition to Sultan Abdülhamid II with the desire to apply it to the cannon he had designed earlier and request that its implementation be allowed. However, all this work and request did not receive the attention they deserved from the State. Here is Ahmed Süreyya Emin Bey's petition dated 29 March 1885:

> When the cannons are fired, a gas emerges in a proportion of from eight percent to ten percent through their touch-holes, creating a light. And because this light also reduces the destination of the cannons and therefore the speed and strength of the cannonballs, the French State has been careful about this important and fearful thing, and last year craftsmen were invited to the invention of a device that prevented the release of this gas. It was heard by your servant a few months ago that a new style of gunpowder chamber cap, which would prevent the emergence of gas leaks that emerged and caused similar problems on the covers of the Krupp cannons, is being investigated by military officers of foreign states. Due to the enthusiasm of this little servant for craftsmanship from birth, I found a solution, even though I was not worthy of the problem mentioned above, by gathering all my ideas on this subject and applying the mental and practical

endeavours that occurred in my youth. Thus, I reached the goal of achieving the invention of the gunpowder chamber cap with the help of Allah, with two new gas rings, one specific to steel and the other to bronze cannons, to prevent gas leaks from the breech with a firing device by blocking the hole. With respect and eagerness, I, slave of our lord, the Sultan, who gives blessings to the world and appreciates the cadres of the precious people, and whose grants were ingrained into the marrow of the members of our family causing us to gain materially and spiritually to the eternal and enormous Ottoman Empire, have dared to present the accurate drawings of the mentioned ring cover and the tool together with the pamphlet on the production, usage, and its benefits to the presence of great hearted majesty. If the supreme ruler deems this correct and apt, and the idea appropriate, it will be applied to cannonballs, one of which is cast in four pounds of steel and the other is cast in the form of a circle, under the supervision of your little servant, and the construction of this is required to be built according to the pictures. At the end of this work, with the support of the ruler, who is the shadow of God on earth, the invention of this little servant can be produced in the Zeytinburnu Royal Steel Factory, and the construction of this invention of your slave can happen with the cannonball stock at hand. In all conditions, the orders and edicts, grace and grant are benefited from the eternal blessings and the benevolence of the kingdom that belongs to the blessings of our Sultan.

Son of Late Emin Bey
(Seal)
Ahmed Süreyya

29 March 1885

The German Krupp Factory owners, who heard about the invention of the ball, immediately rushed to Istanbul. At this time, Alfred Krupp was the head of the Krupp factory. Without the permission of Ahmed Süreyya Emin Bey, Sultan Abdülhamid II gave the plans and drawings of the cannon and the manufacturing drawings to the team of German engineers that had come to him. The German Krupp Factory engineers who received the plans and drawings made the first rapid-fire German cannon two years later and presented a sample to the Sultan, too. This cannon is in the Military Museum [Harbiye, Istanbul] today. In return, Sultan Abdülhamid II gave a cash reward to the Krupp Factory.[15] But he did not bestow even a word of appreciation upon the inventor of the cannon.

After the death of Alfred Krupp in 1887, his son Frederic Krupp, who took over the factory, continued the close relations with the Ottoman Empire. Frederic Krupp's first trip just one month after his father's death was to the Balkans and Istanbul. Istanbul newspapers wrote that Frederic Krupp arrived in Istanbul via Varna on 8 September 1887 to meet Sultan Abdülhamid II.

Zeytinburnu Iron Factory Manufactured First Burst Field Cannon

---

15. Ahmed Süreyya Emin Bey and First Rapid-fire Field Gun, Military Museum and Cultural Site Command Library, Library Sequence no: 620; see also T.N. Eralp in *The Concept of Weapons in Turkish Society throughout History and Weapons Used in the Ottoman Empire*, p. 124.

Metal Label on the Barrel Side of the Burst Field Cannon
Harbiye Military Museum

Ahmed Süreyya Emin Bey and his Burst Field Cannon

This picture is taken from B. Çetin's article "The Ottoman Military Industrial Smokeless Gunpowder Factory during the reign of Abdülhamid II." Devr-i Hamid, Erciyes University Pub., Kayseri, 2011, vol. I, p. 394.

The sales managers of Krupp's arms factories were also with him. The next day, on 9 September, Abdülhamid II met Frederic Krupp after the Friday prayers. The Sultan awarded him medals. On the evening of 12 September, the Sultan invited Frederic Krupp and the delegation to dinner at his residence at Yıldız Palace. The gun manufacturer, who stayed in Istanbul until 16 September, that day met Abdülhamid for the third time during his visit. He left Istanbul after saying goodbye to the Sultan. According to the information in the Ottoman archives, most of the orders for cannons and other military ammunition to the Krupp factory were made during Krupp's visits.

"Süreyya Emin 01: The Manufacturing Inventor of the Imperial Factory, Zeytinburnu" is written on the metal label on the barrel side of the cannon. Next to the cannon are written in Ottoman Turkish and Latin letters "Ahmed Süreyya Emin Efendi, who invented and manufactured the first field cannon in 1866–1868. Birth: 1848 Death: 1923."

MODERN SCIENTIFIC VIEWS IN SUFISM

In this chapter we will look at some of the views of Sufis that were once considered wishful thinking or even absurd, but which have acquired a scientific quality, as attested by the positive sciences of our times. These views are presented today as new discoveries and theories in modern and contemporary science. Actually, they are much older inventions in the ideation, although not at the level of experience and experimentation of modern times, as we shall see.

Panbioism

1. Panbioism and Sufis

One of the ideas of Sufis worth discussing is panbioism. Panbioism says that whatever is in the universe is actually alive. According to this view, everything occurring in nature has soul, mind and will. There is no distinction between beings in the form of living and non-living (organic and inorganic). However, the degree of vitality in beings is different. In some, it is quite high and one can see and perceive it. Others are so low and slow in vitality that it is impossible for a person to be aware of it through naked observation. Mevlana Rumi (d. 1273) expresses this as: "Earth and water, fire and air are alive in the sight of God, even if they seem dead to us."

What humans call "alive" are beings whose vitality they can feel through their external observation. Beings whose vitality is not felt are called "inanimate". Whatever characteristics we call "living beings" have, even though they are in different proportions, non-living beings also have the same characteristics –like life, soul, knowledge, mind and consciousness.

It is said that every being has two kinds of vitality. The first is its apparent vitality. These are the actions necessary for a being to maintain its mere existence, for example, eating and drinking, speaking, moving around and thinking. Sufis also call this "animal life" or "animal vitality". The second is its inherent, deep or inner vitality. This is the metaphysical vitality of beings – that the beings having the knowledge of God's existence consciously and also about worshiping and obeying God. They also call this second vitality "real life" or "human life". These two lives exist in beings in inverse proportion. So, those who have the highest level of apparent life are at the lowest level of inner life. The apparent life of those with the highest degree of inner life is the lowest. For example, although humans have the highest apparent life among all beings, have they the lowest level of inner life. However, it is possible for humans to increase their inner life, if they wish to do so. This requires certain mystical training and knowledge.

> Muhyiddin Ibn Arabi (1164–1240) says:
>
> There is no better creature than inanimate objects. After them come plants in terms of value. After them come sentient animals. However, all of them know with the caliphship (closeness to Allah), (a natural) intuition (discovery), explanation and evidence. As for the creature called Man, it is connected with reason, idea and belief.[16]

---

16. Ibn Arabi, *Fusus al-Hikam* (*The Bezels of Wisdom*), p. 66–67.

He emphasizes that the beings called inanimate are superior to the living things and human beings in terms of true life, that is, in being close to Allah. On the other hand, he also emphasizes that humans have the highest degree of animal life. As a person approaches God, he or she can reach a higher degree in terms of true life. However, they must transcend mental, intellectual and human attachments and boundaries. However, beings other than humans do not have such ties. They are directly close to God with an inner intuition.

> Ibn Arabi expresses the same concept in another work as follows:
>
> In our opinion, everything that is called inanimate or vegetable has its own soul. They are endowed with intellect and perception. Only the people who are capable of discovery (ahl-e-kashf) can understand this.[17]

Here, with the word panbioism, we express that Sufis regard all beings in the universe with an apparent and an inner life, not metaphorically, but truly alive. Modern physics and chemistry have data that supports their views. Before ignoring these, let us consider the origin of this idea of Sufis and how they tried to prove it.

At first sight, there is no doubt that the source of these thoughts of Sufis is the Quran. Because while they are processing these ideas, they take some verses of the Quran as a basis for them. Some of these are as follows:

> The seven heavens, the earth, and all those in them glorify Him. There is not a single thing that does not glorify His praises—but you simply cannot comprehend their glorification.
>
> —Surah Al-Isra, Verse 44

---

17. Ibn Arabi, *Al-Futuhat Al-Makkiyah* (*The Meccan Revelations*), Chapter 23.

> Do you not see that to Allah bow down in submission all those in the heavens and all those on the earth, as well as the sun, the moon, the stars, the mountains, the trees, and all living beings, as well as many humans?
>
> —Surah Al-Hajj, Verse 18

Contrary to the apparent scholars, Sufis take the true meaning of "everything is worshipping Allah" that is mentioned in these and similar verses, and say that everything actually says the name of Allah. They say that in order for something to mention the name of God, first of all, that thing must be alive. While interpreting such verses, apparent scholars such as Al-Zamakhshari (1075–1144) and Beyzavi say that the mention of Allah by beings other than humans is not actual but only with a "language of state", that is, it is metaphorical. Therefore, they do not accept that such inanimate beings need to have abilities such as soul, mind and speech in order to worship. They consider these inanimate objects as they are and consider that they worship the Almighty in their given state only.

By drawing inspiration from the verses of the Quran, Sufis believe that beings other than humans have soul, intelligence, speech and hearing abilities like human beings. Let us now see with what evidence they try to prove this claim, based on their own logical reasoning and mystical experience.

a) *Cosmic worship*

Sufis, based on the verses we mentioned, accept that the whole universe and everything in it worships the Almighty. The logical consequence of this is that they say that everything is truly alive. For example, the great Sufi Ibn Arabi says:

> There is nothing that is not really alive. Except what God reveals, people do not understand their worship...Only the living thing can worship. Therefore, everything is alive.[18]

---
18. Ibn Arabi, *Fusus al-Hikam* (*The Bezels of Wisdom*), p. 213.

b) *Cosmic dance and movement*

According to Sufis, everything from the whole universe to its smallest parts, that is, atoms, are always in an infinite and unlimited motion. This movement is also not accidental; it is harmonious and rhythmic, just like the dance of the dancers who match the music of an orchestra. From the fact that everything is in constant motion in this manner, Sufis conclude that they must be alive like human beings, because moving is one of the qualities of vitality. Mavlana Rumi says:

> O day, arise! The atoms are dancing. The souls are dancing, overcome with ecstasy. I'll whisper in your ear where their dance is taking them. All the atoms in the air and in the desert are insane like us, know this . . .[19]

c) *Eschatological evidence*

Sufis say that according to their religion, since everything will be able to speak and have a speech like us in the hereafter, then this means that everything has a language in this world and can speak. For this reason, Mevlana Rumi says in his book *Fihi Ma Fihi*, "Allah gave speech to us as he gave speech to everything."

d) *Existential (ontological) evidence*

This can be expressed in two ways. First, since everything is from God, everything is the manifestation of God's names and attributes, according to Sufis. Beings exist because God exists. Another name of Allah is "The Ever-Living (Al-Hayy)". Therefore, the manifestation of this name must be seen in all beings. Thus, by the name Al-Hayy of Allah, everything is living and having life.

Second, since there are natural ties and relationships between all beings, and some lives depend on others,

---

19. Mevlana Rumi, *Rubaiyat*, pp. 60–61.

therefore it is not logical to accept some of them alive and not to accept others as such. Everything is essentially the same; their manifestations and appearances are different. For this, if we consider some beings really alive, it is necessary to accept the whole existence alive.

e) *Experiential evidence*

While trying to prove that all beings have life and soul and that they are alive, another evidence that Sufis refer to are the miracles produced by the prophets and some Sufis too. For example, there was the Prophet Solomon's conversation with birds and some animals. Another such example is an event from Prophet Mohammad's (phuh) life. One day when the Prophet was giving sermon in the Madina Mosque, the trunk of the palm tree he used as mihrab (niche in a mosque wall indicating the direction of Mecca) made a sound similar to the voice of a pregnant female camel.[20]

Some conversations of Sufis with animals, trees and stones are also mentioned in this subject. For example, one of them is about Sheikh Abul Qasim Gurgani al-Tusi speaking with a pillar in a mosque.[21]

In this regard, Abu Osman al-Maghribi (d. 983), one of the famous mystics, says, "A person who referred everything to Allah understands the voice of birds and the creaking of the doors with the knowledge of God. They mean to him as translators and signs of God."[22]

With all these evidences, Sufis support their views of panbioism. Let us now explore the value of this view in terms of modern science.

---

20. M.M. Khan, *Sahih al-Bukhari*, II, 26 (I 233, 4 etc.); Ibn Battuta, *Rihla*, vol. I, p. 275; Mevlana Rumi, *Masnavi*, vol. I, 2112; AliAl-Hujwiri, *Kashf al-Mahjub*, p. 234.
21. Hujwiri, p. 234.
22. Al-Baqli, *Tafsir*, XXVII, 16, V. 278a (Berlin); Mansur Al-Hallaj, *Kitab al-Tawasin*, p. 128.

2. Panbioism and Modern Science

Even if scientists claim about some of their inventions as novel, it is seen that rather than coming up with completely new things, most of the times the ever-developing science prove the historically old ideas – only in a more scientific manner with the opportunities provided by new developments. Advances in chemistry, biology and astrophysics over the last 50–100 years prove the accuracy of the panbioism view. Let's try to explain this with a few examples.

Quantum, relativity, and subatomic theories have changed many of the fundamental concepts of classical physics based on the Aristotelian–Newtonian tradition, such as time, space, motion and matter. Quantum mechanics has shown that the separation of matter into organic and inorganic forms is now only a traditional and conceptual distinction. It is a fact that subatomic particles communicate, liaise, decide and exchange ideas with one another just like living things. No living creature can show this voluntary movement which these subatomic particles show. They can move so fast that within a millionth of a second, a particle can exchange information with another particle as far away as a galaxy.[23] Therefore, it can be said that all beings have an active life at the level of atoms and subatomic particles.

On the other hand, research like that of German chemist and physicist Friedrich Wöhler brought new conviction that inorganic matter is organic in chemistry and biology. In 1928 he obtained urea or $CO(NH_2)_2$, found in the urine, by separating the chemical ammonium cyanate, considered to be inanimate till then, in water and evaporating the solution. This clearly showed that the inanimate are alive. Earlier, it was believed that urea could only be obtained from live kidneys. Especially after 1945, many synthetics eliminated

---

23. G. Zukav, *The Dancing Wu Li Masters*, p. 72.

the inorganic separation of live acids from the scene. In fact, it had been already shown by Lavoisier and Berzelius that carbon is the basic substance of every living thing and that carbon itself has the characteristic of being alive, and the differentiation between animate and inanimate was thus somewhat reduced.

Detailed observations further confirm the view of the Sufis about panbioism. For example, the growth of a diamond that was examined by the British scientist Nelson in the laboratory is one of the closest proofs of this, an observation that was also the subject of the news of BBC Television on the evening of 10 August 1983 at 9 o'clock, surprised many people. In a similar fashion, there was news of the discovery by the Western scientists in July 1988 that water has memory and recollection like living things. This news was broadcasted on radio in Turkey also. We can be sure that these and similar new discoveries and observations, which will occur in the future, will once again prove to us more clearly the old views of the Sufis that everything has a life and intelligence.

3. Panbioism and Similar Philosophical Views

Some people may liken panbioism to some philosophical views. These are doctrines such as panpsychism, vitalism and hylozoism. Although there are some apparent similarities between them with panbioism, there are some fundamental differences too. Let's take a look at these aspects.

4. Panbioism and Panpsychism

We can trace the foundations of panpsychism in some ways to Pythagoreanism, especially to Stoicism. The greatest similarity is that the Stoics also explain the origin of everything in what they call the "Universal Soul" or the "Universal Mind" and thus say that everything has a soul.

The following words from the Stoic Zeno show this:

> There is nothing that is not made of life and mind. The universe produces life and rational beings. Therefore, the universe itself is composed of mind and life.[24]

But these ancient panpsychist philosophers regarded soul and mind as matter at the same time, so their panpsychism is a form of materialism. In this respect, too, this similarity between panpsychism and panbioism of the Sufis is an apparent and formal similarity. Because the spirit and the mind, which are foreseen as the principle of life and being alive in panbioism, are not themselves material, but the manifestation of the Al-Hayy (Ever-Living) attribute of God. This, too, is the most important difference.

However, modern panpsychism of philosophers, psychologists, and scientists such as F.C.S. Schiller, A. Schopenhauer, G.T. Feshner, P. Teilhard de Chardin, and C.H. Waddington have closer resemblances with panbioism because, like the Sufis, they do not reduce the soul and the principle of life to matter, and on the other hand, they more explicitly argue that inorganic matter has life and will. For example, Schopenhauer says:

> I am the first to argue that everything vital and inorganic must be qualified by will. Because, although it has been thought that will is the attribute of perception and therefore of life until now; it has been understood with me that life itself is the manifestation of will.[25]

Contrary to his claim, Schopenhauer confirms that although he is not the first to attribute will to everything, Sufis see will and discernment in everything. It should not be forgotten that modern panpsychist thinkers, most of them German, may have been influenced by Mevlana Rumi through Goethe. In particular, there are similarities

---

24. Cicero, *On the Nature of the Gods*, See. II, Sec. VIII.
25. A. Schopenhauer, *On the Will in Nature*, p. 309.

between Feshner's typical expressions on this subject and Mevlana Rumi's. This modern panpsychism is the closest to panbioism among other similar doctrines.

5. Panbioism, Animism and Vitalism

Let us first state that the animism which concerns the history of religions and wants to explain the origin of religion, has nothing to do with us here. The animism we are talking about here is philosophical animism. The aspect of this doctrine that resembles panbioism is that it accepts that everything is composed of soul and body; but by treating the body itself as inanimate, it differs from panbioism.

Vitalism, a doctrine close to philosophical animism, sees the life of living organisms as the psyche (spirit). This vitalism, which has become a complete metaphysical doctrine with Bergson, actually has no resemblance to panbioism because it is, above all, a doctrine that belongs only to living beings. By accepting the principle of life outside of matter and arguing that it is not dependent on matter, it differs from panbioism. According to panbioism, life itself is not a principle, but a manifestation. There is no distinction between soul and body. Biologism, which is another variant of vitalism and which reduces all life phenomena to the mechanics of physics–chemistry phenomena, is fundamentally different from panbioism. In short, vitalism, regardless of its type, is a doctrine that is only about living beings. In this respect, it differs from panbioism in terms of scope and purpose.

6. Panbioism and Hylozoism

A doctrine closer to panbioism than vitalism and animism is hylozoism. According to this old doctrine of the Miletus school, the essence of everything is water or air, and everything is alive. As such, it has a lot to do with panbioism. But according to this doctrine, the fact that everything is alive is not literal, but only verbal and metaphorical.[26] If that is the case, then fundamentally panbioism differs from it. In addition, some historians of contemporary philosophy state that what we understand with hylozoism today has nothing to do with the philosophers of Miletus, and calling these doctrines hylozoism is wrong.[27]

Converting One Element into Another or Converting Copper into Gold

Until recently, this idea, which alchemists and Sufis had many years ago, was regarded as a daydream, fraud and quackery. But today this is a proven scientific fact as well. Humanity saw its reality as obvious, but painful, in Hiroshima.

Archaeological excavations and anthropological data show us that people have had an excessive attachment to gold since ancient times. The reason for this is the durability of this material, its bright and heart-warming colour, as well as its use as ornaments and money. The scarcity of gold in nature compared to other mines increased its value even more.

All these properties of gold had led people we call alchemists to try to obtain gold by artificial means since ancient times. However, it should be noted that people fell in love with gold not only for its properties –there was another reason. And that reason was the possibility of this idea becoming a reality. Humans have long thought about the existence of the universe surrounding them and the emergence of various beings, including matter. In China, Babylon and ancient Egypt they thought that all mines and metals emerged from a single ore, and the difference

---

26. P. Edwards, "Panpsychism", *The Encyclopaedia of Philosophy*, vol. VI, p. 23.
27. W.K.C. Guthier, *A History of Greek Philosophy*, vol. I, p. 67; J. Burnet, *Early Greek Philosophy*, p. 12 footnote 3.

between them was a difference in appearance and quality. Later, Aristotle was of the opinion that the formation of minerals happened due to the compression of humid and dry air beneath the soil. He thought that matter was formed by the compression of the humid air and the hard and solid minerals were formed by the compression of dry air.

But more scientific views on this issue were put forward by Islamic chemists. It is possible to collect these views into two different schools of thought. The first is the school of Jabir ibn Hayyan. According to Jabir ibn Hayyan, all minerals and metals consist of the mixture of two basic elements in various proportions –sulphur and mercury. However, what Jabir meant by sulphur and mercury – although this issue is still controversial –was not sulphur and mercury as we know them, which are elements themselves. Although his elements were named as such, they represented the two fundamental natural forces from which all the elements and metals (including sulphur and mercury as we know them) come from. All elements and minerals emerged in nature as a result of the physical and chemical change of these two main elements. This view of Jabir was a popular view for many years both in the East and the West, until the 18th century.

The second school is the school represented by chemists and alchemists such as Abul Qasim Muhammed bin Ahmed as-Simavi (13th century), who is famous as Al-Iraki. According to this school, minerals and elements were the result of the evolution or metamorphosis of a naturally occurring mineralizing force, which they often called "Al-Iksir".

These Islamic chemists, including the chemist Sufis, who formed two different schools about the formation of elements and metals, converged on one basic idea. This idea was that the transformation of elements and metals was possible. So, as a logical consequence of this, if one wanted and was capable of it, the person could convert one metal into another. For this reason, many Islamic chemists, especially Sufis, argued that it was possible to obtain gold by artificial means, especially from the types of metals closest to gold, like copper. In some sources, it was also said that some of them had experimented on this subject and eventually even achieved their goals.

Whether it was true or not, the rumour was that they actually turned copper into gold; what was true in this respect was their basic thoughts, once regarded as trickery and purely fanciful that one element could be transformed into another. According to today's science of nuclear chemistry, their dreams were a scientific truth. This fact, put forward by physicists and chemists working hand-in-hand with the chemical changes of atomic nuclei, can be summarized as follows in the language of science today:

The essence of the transformation is to change the charge and mass of the atom by rearranging the nucleus of the atom by external interventions for example, by using high temperatures, high pressures and catalysts. If this is in terms of simpler chemical reactions based on the exchange of electrons, the change occurs at the level of atom, molecule and ion, and not in the nucleus. In this process, a major conversion is not achieved at this level. For major element-level transformation, modifications should be made in the nucleus. These modifications can be provided by using protons, neutrons, deuterons (heavy hydrogen isotope), alpha particles (helium-4 nucleus) and ions of light elements such as boron, oxygen, neon and argon. When these particles are given special speeds and the nucleus to be changed is bombarded with them, the bombarded nucleus changes in mass and charge, and transforms into a new a new element.

For example, let's show how helium is made from lithium by proton bombardment:

$$_3^7 Li + p \rightarrow 2\ _2^4 He + d$$

p: Proton   d: Deuteron

The number at the top of the symbol indicates the atomic mass of the nucleus and the number at the bottom indicates the charge of the nucleus.

In this way, helium is obtained from lithium. Thus, it has been established how real and scientific the old dreams are today.

Gold can be obtained from any element in the same manner. However, according to the currently available techniques, since the cost to make is Kayseri many times higher than the value of the gold obtained, nobody is engaged in this business.

Before concluding, let us mention a view closely related to the subject, which Sufis foretold long ago. Long before modern science, the Sufis said that the atom could be split and talked of the existence of subatomic particles.

It has been accepted since ancient times that the universe contained tiny particles called atoms. This is commonly called atomism. Historians of science and thought differ on the origin of atomism. Some argue that it was born in Indian thought for the first time and then moved to the Middle East and Greece, while others held the opposite view – according to them, it was born in Greece for the first time and passed to other countries from there. Regardless of the opinion on this issue, we see that some of the Muslim thinkers had adopted atomism as of the 8th century. However, they interpreted this in different ways in line with their own personal views and brought a new understanding to the thought. Some Sufis, such as Mevlana Rumi, accepted for the first time that the atom could be split. As is known, earlier atomists, whether Muslim or Greek, believed that the atom was indivisible and described the atom as the smallest unit that could not be further fragmented.

However, Mevlana Rumi clearly stated that the atom could be broken down. He said:

> If you cut an atom,
>
> A sun in the middle
>
> And around the sun too,
>
> You find planets that rotate continuously.

Taking into account the scientific and technological inadequacy of that period, we could not expect the author of these sentences, which symbolically express a scientific truth, to demonstrate it experimentally. However, this statement from him more than enough to be accepted as revolutionary for that period in terms of expressing a scientific truth.

A New Creation at Every Moment or the Cosmic Dance

Sufis have a theory that they call "re-creation." Its essence is this: The being is renewed and changes every moment. There is a new creation at every moment. This renewal movement is the essence of being.

The principle of this renewal movement was in the form of an existence (permanence) and extinction (annihilation). The being undergoes existence at a time and then annihilation in a permanent form and in continuity. This continuous movement of existence and extinction also brings innovation to the being. There is no repetition in the universe. Thus, one being is not exactly the same as another being. The moment of annihilation is so short that an existence immediately takes its place at its end. That is why people are not aware of the continual annihilation. The changes that can be observed in entities arise as a result of these changes that occur over a long period, and which cannot be observed with the naked eye.

Sufis reveal these views by taking inspiration from the following verse of the Quran as well as based on their own intuition:

> He is in a new job every day.
>
> —Surah Rahman 29

This verse is explained by the apparent scholars by saying that Allah appropriates every moment in the universe or creates a being every moment. However, the Sufis, without denying this possible meaning of the verse, go further and put forward a new meaning, which we have summarized above and which they call "re-creation". Thus, Sufis pursue a very rich and dynamic understanding of the universe with the theory of recreation every moment.

Mevlana Rumi stated in the following verses that the whole universe died one moment and was revived in the next:

> Every moment the world is renewed,
>
> And we, seemingly remain the same,
>
> We are not aware that it has been renewed.
>
> Although there is a continuation of the like
>
> Life is always flowing into newness like a river.[28]

Many such expressions have been expressed by many Sufis, from Al-Ghazali to Dawud al-Qaysari, from Ibn al-Farid to Saadi Shirazi.

---

28. Mevlana Rumi, *Masnavi*, Vol. I, 1143–1146.

Sufis associate the death and resurrection of the being at every moment and the emergence of each resurrection as a new being, with the manifestation of Allah, with Allah's names and attributes. Allah renews the existence in every manifestation, as well as creating new beings; the beings that we see as old are actually being renewed. Therefore, the Sufis also call the theory of re-creation as "manifestation". However, there is a point to be made here. Manifestation has two meanings according to Sufis. The first is that God gives information in the form of inspiration and intuition to the hearts of chaste servants. We can call this "epistemological" (informational) manifestation. This has nothing to do with the theory of re-creation. The second manifestation is what we can call an "ontological" (existential) manifestation. It has the same meaning as the theory of re-creation.

In particular, today's atomic physics and conceptions in cosmology are moving towards these re-creation theories of the Sufis. At the level of subatomic particles, the functioning of the universe and its structure are completely identical to these views of the Sufis. The Sufis thus put forward a description of the modern cosmological view many years ago.

Today, it is known that all atoms, and therefore every entity, consist of three particles with mass and one particle without mass. The three particles with mass are proton, neutron and electron. The particle without mass is the photon, which represents the electromagnetic radiation unit. There is also an anti-particle for each particle.

Protons, electrons, and photons are stationary; however, excluding the situation where they can enter into a course of collisions and encounters in which they can disappear. But in contrast, the neutron is naturally constantly shifting. This moving displacement is called "beta distortion (beta detail)".

This beta distortion is the basis of a kind of radioactivity that allows the neutron to turn into a proton, bringing with it an electron and a new kind of mass-less particle called a neutrino.

According to the quantum–relativity theory of particles, there is an electromagnetic interplay between electrons and photons on the one hand, and a gravitational interplay on the other hand. All these interactions and attractions push the subatomic particle into a vibration and a subatomic dance. After all, the whole universe is in a vibration at the subatomic level. In most of the course of collisions caused by high physical energy, strong electromagnetic and weak inter-particle interactions can produce a complex chain of events. Often, the original collided particles disappear and new particles emerge. These either get into a new collision or break down. Sometimes they eventually turn into stationary particles so that they survive. Meanwhile, many unstable particles live for less than a millionth of a second, and then disappear.

Therefore, to put it briefly, these subatomic particles that constitute the atom are not separate from one other; rather, they form an inseparable dynamic unity of intermediate interactions and attractions. These intermediate interactions provide a continuous flow of energy into a wide variety of particle samples in a rhythmic natural motion. In this rhythmic motion, particles exist and disappear continually. Thus, the universe is in an infinite movement. This movement of subatomic particles is never the same. As the Feynman diagrams show, every subatomic motion is expressed by the sudden disappearance of essential particles. And this, in our opinion, is nothing more than what our Sufis mean with the theory of "sudden re-creation" or "manifestation".

Since the Sufis did not have the resources and opportunities to express this scientific truth in a different manner at that time, they likened it to the vibration that occurs in the being, as if by the effect of the breathing that God used to say "Be" to create it, and so they symbolized it. However, they clearly emphasized that many people would not understand this still, whenever they talked about this. This is what Ibn Arabi said:

> How beautiful are God's words about the universe and its change in a single essence and a new creation according to divine breaths! His saying about a single being is also related to the whole universe. No, they are in a new creation suit. They (people) do not understand the renewal of the creative order according to breaths.[29]

The Multi-Universe Idea

For a long time, it was common among Muslims, especially among Sufis, to say "He is the prophet of eighteen thousand realms, even one hundred thousand realms" in order to exemplify and exalt our Prophet. The majority, except for some of the Sufis, did not really mean to say that there was more than one realm or that it was not a single but a multi-universe. Some people say this as they hear it, without thinking about its meaning. Some interpret it to mean that there may be eighteen thousand different types of beings in our present universe, or that there are many orders of entities. Therefore, they interpret the expression eighteen thousand worlds or realms in a figurative sense.

However, some Sufis accepted that there were universes and worlds other than our universe and our world, in real terms. They pointed out that there was not one universe,

---

29. Ibn Arabi, *Fusus al-Hikam* (*The Bezels of Wisdom*), pp. 153–154.

but many universes. Therefore, they predicted that not one, but multiple solar systems and galaxies filled the space. Today's astronomers and cosmographers confirm this to be correct.

According to our understanding, there are signs supporting these views of Sufis and scientists in both the Quran and Hadiths. For instance, the following verse is very meaningful and interesting:

> It is God who created seven heavens, and a similar number of earths. His command descends through them, so that you may know that God is able to do all things, and that God's knowledge has encompassed all things.
>
> —Surah At-Talaq, Verse 12

The following Hadith is also very interesting:

> O God! Lord of the seven heavens and all their shadows, Lord of the seven earths and all that they bear . . .[30]

The expressions "seven heavens" and "seven earths" in both the verse and the Hadith clearly show us that there are more than one world and heaven in space. This can be seven or more. Because, according to what Lisan al-Arab and Tajul Arus report, the word "seven" in Arabic does not only mean the number seven, but also means "multitude".

These verses and Hadiths with similar meanings attracted the attention of commentators and other Islamic scholars in the past. But since these people were under the influence of Ptolemaic astronomy, they did not think of such statements in a way that could infer that there could be universes and systems other than ours. As it is known, according to Ptolemy astronomy, the sky was considered as consisting of seven layers.

---

30. M.M. Khan, *Sahih al-Bukhari*, Oppressions: 13; Al-Qurtubi, *Tafsir*, vol. 18, p. 175.

For example, as al-Qurtubi narrates, the ancients used the terms "seven heavens" and "seven earths" either as the seven layers of the heavens and the earth, or as planets known only as seven at that time, or they interpreted it as seven different main types of existence in the sky and the earth, consisting of the realm of angels, the realm of jinn, the world of devils, the world of minerals, the world of plants, the world of animals and the human world.[31]

There are other verses that indicate that there may be many separate solar systems. Two of these are:

> I swear by the Lord of the East and the West.
> —Surah al-Ma'arij, Verse 40
>
> Praise be to the Lord of the Worlds.
> —Surah al-Fatiha, Verse 1

Ancient scholars gave different meanings to the words "east (plural)", "west (plural)" and "worlds". They said that in plural expressions such as east and west, diverse climatic zones and countries' own east and west are expressed. Likewise, the world and the hereafter or different types of beings are expressed in plural terms. Maybe these verses contain these meanings as well. But this also does not mean that these verses necessarily indicate the presence of more than one world or different worlds. Yet it is also possible that the sun of the solar system of every world rises and sets according to certain principles.

Five years ago [that is, in the year 1983], I gave a lecture in London on "Many Solar Systems in Islam" in the light of similar verses and Hadiths that we have mentioned here, inspired by the view of the Sufis of the possibility of multi-universes. My talk was similar to what I have written here. This caused some reactions from some people. But this view is gaining support from many scientists these days.

---

31. Al-Qurtubi, *Tafsir*, p. 173–177.

Another point expressed in the Quran is about expansion of spaces:

> We built the sky with our hands; we are certainly extenders.
>
> —Surah Az-Zariyat, Verse 47

Many commentators in the past and even modern writers could not give the meaning of this verse accurately. This is because they have explained the word "musi'un" used in the verse by giving it a more general and, in a sense, ambiguous meaning, saying that Allah is the owner of the great power or the possessor of greatness. This has happened since they do not have any idea that the universe can expand or be expansive.

However, if we consider the last part of the verse – "we are surely extenders"– by relating it with the beginning of the verse – "we set the sky with our hands" – it becomes necessary to give a more specific meaning and this word. "We are certainly extenders" means we are expanders of the sky, that is, space. Such a meaning is quite logical and scientific today. Since 1917, especially with the work of astronomer Willem de Sitter, we can think of space in an expansive capacity. With scientists such as E. Hubble, Abbe Lemaitre and Arthur Eddington, the phenomenon of the expansion of space has become a purely scientific view.

Another verse that strengthens the meaning we have given to this verse and points out that the space has been made expanding is this:

> All praise is for Allah, the creator of the heavens and the earth; it is Allah who made the angels two, three or four winged messengers. Allah increases in creation whatever He wills. Surely Allah is most capable of everything.
>
> —Surah Fatir, Verse 1

The Possibility of Overcoming Time and Space/ Relativity and Destructibility of Time and Space

Finally, the issue we want to focus on is the issue of acceptance by the Sufis that the boundaries of time and space can be transcended and that they can go beyond time and space. In other words, it is a matter of "passing of time" and "passing of space".

Those who read or listen to the stories of Awliya know that a saint (wali) has been seen at the same time in two separate venues, or that a saint crosses a river by walking on water. Let us put aside the question of whether this or that saint could actually have experienced these events, which are described as miracles in reference to the saints, and dwell on the fact that what they express conveys a truth. This truth is that time and space are relative, and therefore they can be transcended and surpassed – it is the destructibility of time and space dimension.

Many philosophers and scientists from the East and the West, from Abu Bakr al-Razi to Aristotle, from Al-Farabi to Kant, regarded time and space either as a mental and intellectual phenomenon or as a physical and existential phenomenon. They regarded them as having existence, meaning a fact or a type of being that has absolute existence, separate from and independent of human beings. The prevailing view was that no physical or metaphysical event was conceivable without taking into account the factors of time and space. Humans had to stay confined to these in an absolute sense.

However, the concepts of time and space, like many concepts of classical and medieval physics and philosophy, were shaken at their roots along with A. Einstein's general and specific theories of relativity. In fact, even before

Einstein, some philosophers and scientists such as Al-Kindi (796–866) also thought that time and space were arbitrary or relative.[32] But the mathematical expression of this belongs to Einstein. With this theory, it was established that time and space were not absolute, but relative. Sufis had expressed this long ago with their concept of passing of time and passing of space. And if we believe the stories and anecdotes about them that they were seen in two separate places at the same time, which are a fact, we can say that they have lived and experienced the phenomenon personally.

Sufis explain that this idea of passing of time and passing of space, or going beyond time and space and ignoring them, is actually possible as a logical consequence of the relativity theory as follows: When a person has real and true knowledge (because of god's blessing), the person becomes a "saver" in the universe like Khidr; so it goes before, beyond and above time and space.[33]

Here, it would be appropriate to briefly explain what Sufis understand with the notion of "saving".

Saving is the Sufis' possession of real knowledge and, thanks to this, learning the rules and customs of the universe, and with the help of them showing and experiencing events that are considered unusual or extraordinary for us. But these are actually normal in terms of the rules of the universe. But because people have yet to discover and use those rules normally, they seem extraordinary to them. When the hidden secrets, rules and customs of the universe are discovered gradually, most of them will appear as common or in other words, scientific facts. However, there are Sufis who can

---

32. M. Bayrakdar, "Relativity and Similarities According to al-Kindi and Einstein", *Science and Technology*, issue 153, 1980, pp. 10–12.
33. Dawud al-Qaysari, *Tahqîqu Mâ'i'l-Hayât ve Keşfu Esrâri'z-Zulumât*, Turkish translation by M. Bayrakdar, *Dawud from Kayseri*, pp. 61–63.

anticipate and know them with their intuition and intellectual knowledge. Here, let us record the following quote from Sadr al-Din al-Qunawi:

> The Messenger of Allah (pbuh) said, "If you knew the Truth in the full sense, you would have walked on water, the mountains would slide with you."

Especially in this Hadith, finding the state of extinction is pointed out. In short, it means this: if you could become extinct in the existence of the truth and then find permanence with it, you would have saved against everything, especially in terms of invention and destruction.[34]

This Hadith, which Sadr al-Din al-Qunawi mentioned and interpreted, gives information about the ideas of the Sufis. They also base their ideas on many historical facts mentioned by the Quran. Let us first mention a few verses addressing the thoughts that show that time and space are relative. For example, it is stated in the following verses that time is nominal, relative and comparative:

> Truly, a day with your Lord is like a thousand years from what you will count.
>
> —Surah Ta-ha, Verse 104

> They want punishment from you quickly. Allah will never deter their threat. A day with your Lord is like a thousand years from what you count.
>
> —Surah Al-Haj, Verse 47

> Angels and spirit ascend to the Lord within a day, the amount of which lasts for fifty thousand years.
>
> —Surah Al-Ma'arij, Verse 4

The historical events that are described in the following verses clearly show that such events and savings were possible before and now can happen:

---

34. Sadr al-Din al-Qunawi, *al-Hadisu'l-Erba'in*, Turkish translation by A. Akçiçek, p. 38.

Solomon asked, "O chiefs! Which of you can bring me the queen's throne before they come to me in full submission?" One mighty jinn responded, "I can bring it to you before you rise from this council of yours. And I am quite strong and trustworthy for this task." But the one who had knowledge of the Book said, "I can bring it to you in the blink of an eye." So when Solomon saw it placed before him, he exclaimed, "This is by the grace of my Lord to test me whether I am grateful or ungrateful."

—Surah An-Naml, Verse 38–40

As it can be understood, in these verses, it is stated that the throne of Bilqis, the queen of Sheba, was brought to the Prophet Solomon in the blink of an eye and that the one who brought it was someone who knew the knowledge of the "Book". This person was one of the most powerful devils and jinn (Ifrit). He brought the throne of Bilqis, which was at a distance of two months if it was brought on foot, in a blink of an eye. Although there are those who say that this person was Khidr or Prophet Solomon himself, the majority of commentators accept that it was one of the companions of Prophet Solomon. Even Ibn Arabi says, "This person is said to be the vizier of the Prophet Solomon named Asif ibn Barkhiya." Therefore, as Sufis say, the boundaries of time and space do not matter for a person who has real knowledge (the knowledge of the Book). Whoever has this knowledge can transcend time and space. As Ibn Arabi says, for such people, "Time is of imaginary nature that does not have a real existence."[35]

---

35. Ibn Arabi, *Al-Futuhat Al-Makkiyah*, C. II, p. 458; See also. M. Bayrakdar, "Cosmological Relativity of Ibn Arabi", *Islamic Culture*, C. 58, No: 1984, p. 248.

The Divine Light of Prophet Mohammad and Energy

Almost all Sufis admit that the universe does not consist of what the philosophers call "Prima Materia" or First Matter, or what the theologians call "Absence". According to them, a tenet they call "Divine Light of Mohammad" is the essence of the universe. According to this, God first created the light of the Prophet from God's own Divine Light, and from it all other beings, from angels to human beings, were created in a descending chain-like order. Sufis sometimes call this Divine Light of Mohammad as Soul of Mohammad, First Intelligence, or Universal Soul. The fact that this Divine Light, which is the metaphysical basis of the universe, means light and energy in the cosmological and physical sense had been proposed only by Sufis only such as Dawud al-Qaysari. Accordingly, the essence of the universe and the essence of matter is energy. Nature is nothing but energy. This is expressed quite clearly with the following statement of Dawud al-Qaysari: "Nature is the general total energy, which has a luminous and burning feature."[36] As a matter of fact, Henry Corbin also noted that Dawud of Kayseri defined the concept of nature as general energy.[37]

> Then God turned towards the heaven which (for that time) was like smoke (or gas), saying to it and to the earth, "Submit, willingly or unwillingly." They both responded, "We submit willingly."
>
> —Surah Fussilat, Verse 11

Dawud al-Qaysari interprets the word "smoke" in the verse as amorphous energy and accepts that the essence of

---

36. Dawud al-Qaysari, 'Introduction', *Matla' Khususi'l-Kelim fi Ma'ani Fusus al-Hikam*, Bombay, 1881. p. 22.
37. H. Corbin, *L'Imagination Créatrice dans le Soufisme d'Ibn Arabi*, p. 228.

everything is energy.[38] However, he doesn't go deeper into the concept of this energy.

Like Dawud al-Qaysari, modern German chemist and philosopher Wilhelm Ostwald has argued more systematically in his book *Die Energie* (1908) that in a cosmological sense, the essence of physical nature is energy, not matter. This view of his has been called cosmological energetism. In addition, the famous physicist Helmholtz removed the concept of force from the principles of mechanics and replaced it with energy. Thus, he explained the reason for the physical-mechanical changes with energy. Thus, the change in the state of matter and its assumption of various forms does not originate from matter itself as dialectical materialists claim, rather it is scientifically explained by energy, which is a principle beyond matter. This is a radical refutation of materialism, because matter, which is claimed as a principle in itself, is no longer a principle and is replaced by energy. That is why Lenin harshly accuses Wilhelm Ostwald of being "pure idealist".

Eye of the Heart or Sinoatrial Node

Some Sufis, especially Al-Ghazali, say that humans have an inner eye just like their outer eyes and they give it the name "Eye of the Heart". Our outer eyes are at the exterior of the body, and the inner eye is inside the body, in fact, it is in the heart. The Eye of the Heart has all the functions that the outer eyes perform. Just as the outer eyes enable a person to see and perceive their outer world, the Eye of the Heart enables a person to see their inner or their spiritual world. In addition, this eye, which Sufis call the Eye of the Heart, has other characteristics of its own. Despite being a beatific tiny

---

38. Dawud al-Qaysari, *Matla' Khususi'l-Kelim fi Ma'ani Fusus al-Hikam*, p. 262.

organ in the heart, it cannot be seen with the naked eye. It can only be seen with a microscope. The main source of life is in this eye. The true human soul is located at this point in the heart.

There are two types of souls according to Sufis. The first is the animal soul; its place is the liver. The second is the true soul; its place is in the heart – actually, in the heart of the eye. The main source of life is this heart's eye. It is loaded with energy and electricity. The whole body gets its electricity from it. When its electricity runs out, the whole body dies. Before seeing how this thing that Sufis call the Eye of the Heart is explained in modern science, let's tell you what the great Sufi and philosopher Al-Ghazali said about it.

Al-Ghazali mentions the Eye of the Heart in many of his books.[39] In his famous work, *Al-Risatu'l-Leddunya* he says:

> Some of the Sufis said, "Like the body, the heart also has an eye. Man sees the visible things with the eyes of the head and the invisible truths with the eyes of the heart." Our Prophet (pbuh) said, "Every human's heart has two eyes. He can grasp the unseen with his eyes. If Allah wishes good for a servant, He opens his heart's eyes so that he can see what his eyes cannot see."[40]

The "Third Eye", or "Spiritual Eye", or "Spiritual Heart" which is referred by the Sufis is found in the physical organ that is in the heart, along with the true soul as mentioned earlier. Until recently, this Spiritual Heart, or Heart's Eye, was viewed only as a metaphysical concept. Some scholars claimed that this was a purely spiritual thing and in fact there was no such "Eye" in reality. The Sufis, on the other

---

39. Al-Ghazali, *Ihya' Ulum al-Din*, Vol. I, pp. 49, 78-79; Vol. II, p. 239; Vol. III, pp. 7, 15; Vol. IV, pp. 24, 363-364; Al-Ghazali, *Mustafa Fi Usul ud-din*, pp. 22-23; Al-Ghazali, *Mishkat al-Anwar*, pp. 119, 131, 136, 138.
40. Al-Ghazali, *Al-Risatu'l-Leddunya*, Turkish translation by A. Şener and Ş. Topaloğlu, *Divine Secret*, pp. 18-19.

Modern Scientific Views in Sufism

hand, argued that there was such an eye in the heart, but its functions were spiritual and metaphysical.

Around 1938, two anatomists, Sir A. Keith, an Englishman, and J. Flack, a Scotsman, discovered a point in the heart which was as the Sufis had described. This point is sometimes referred in medicine as "Keith-Flack" or the name of these two anatomists who discovered it and sometimes as Sinoatrial Node. This point, invisible to the eye but seen with a microscope, is located at the top of the heart at the junction of the vena cava and the right atrium. This point, which provides the involuntary movement of the heart, emits light and energy in the body with a continuous movement, that flashes every second, like the flashing light of an ambulance or fire truck. If this light goes out completely, the person dies. The internal electricity to the heart and body is provided by this. It was not incorrect for Sufis to describe the heart as "light" for this reason.

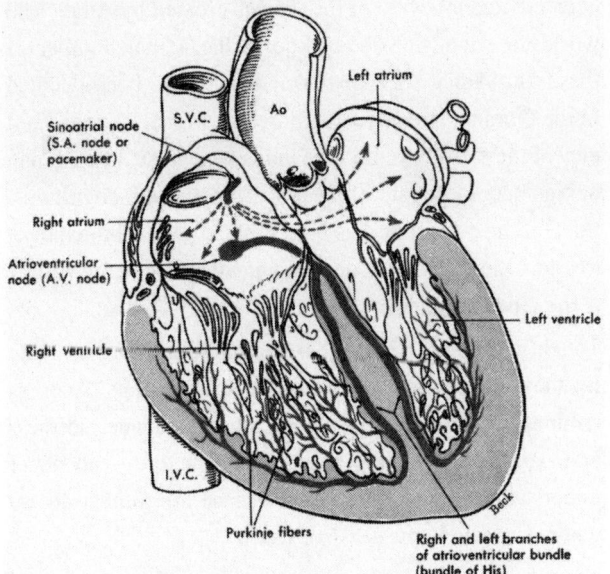

Sinoatrial node (Eye of the Heart) and the electrical system of the heart

Organic Information Theory and Human Embryological Development

Al-Ghazali made a very interesting point in his book titled *Al-Munqidh min al-dalal*. He talked about parallelism between the stages of human embryological development and the ways and means of obtaining information. This showed that the types of knowledge that are different in nature and character are a function of each organ of the human being and as a result, Al-Ghazali tried to establish a theory of knowledge that we can call Organic Knowledge Theory. In doing so, Al-Ghazali, perhaps for the first time among scholars, accurately described the embryological development of human beings.

> First, let us cite Al-Ghazali's own words on the subject:
>
> It is necessary to know that humans are actually devoid of knowledge by the virtue of their creation. They have been created unaware of the worlds created by Allah. The worlds are many. Nobody knows the actual number of these, but Allah. As a matter of fact, it has been decreed in the Quran, "Nobody can know the armies of your Lord except the Lord" (Surah Al-Muddassir, Verse 31). Human beings become aware of these worlds through cognitions. Each of the cognitions has been created so that humans get to know the world of beings. What we mean by the worlds is the types of beings.
>
> Touch is the first feeling that is created in humans. With it, they understand the properties of beings such as coldness, warmth, dryness, moistness, old age, softness and hardness. With the sense of touch, they can never understand colours and sounds. These are almost absent when it comes to the sense of touch.
>
> Then the sense of sight is created in them. They understand colours and shapes with it. This is the largest in the world of feelings.

Then the sense of hearing develops in them. It makes them hear voices and tunes.

Then the feeling of taste is created. Thus, humans can penetrate the world of feelings (with all these). Then, when they approach the age of seven, the power to distinguish develops in them. Thus, the human body enters a new phase. With this, the humans understand some new things that are not in world of feelings and are more than this world.

Then (humans) enters a new development phase. The power to reason develops in them. They understand what is required and what is permissible with the use of their mind. They also perceive things that were not found in them in the previous periods.

There is another period beyond the mind, where another eye (Eye of the Heart) opens. The humans see the unseen with it, understand future events and some things that the mind is incapable of understanding.[41]

Thus, according to Al-Ghazali, knowledge is a matter of feeling first. It is the sense organs that provide this. These are, in order of priority, the skin, eyes, ears and tongue. Knowledge, then, is a matter of discernment and reasoning. The brain and nerve organs provide this. After all, knowledge is a matter of seeing through the eyes of the heart. The Eye of the Heart in the heart organ provides this. According to Al-Ghazali, persons act only with their feelings until they are seven years old, and their knowledge is the information provided by these feelings. Then the functions of the brain begin to develop. The forces and faculties that we call reason and discernment are formed. With these, people start to think in the real sense. Mental knowledge is also added to the emotional knowledge. Later, if one makes the necessary effort, one gets free from the passion of feelings and if one

---

41. Al-Ghazali, *Al-Munqidh min al-dalal*, pp. 41–42.

is able to overcome the limitations of the mind, one can manage the functions of the Eye of the Heart. Thus, a person can obtain inspirational or intuitive knowledge besides and beyond sensory and mental knowledge. Al-Ghazali calls the first-degree knowledge "sensations" or "needs", which are obtained through feelings. He calls second-degree knowledge "permissible", which is obtained by reason. He gives the name of the third-degree knowledge "knowledge", "" or "discovered knowledge", which is obtained by the Eye of the Heart.

According to Al-Ghazali, knowledge of feelings alone is not enough; it must be supported with the knowledge of the mind. The knowledge of the mind is not enough by itself; it must be supported by the knowledge of the heart. Our knowledge consists of certain functions of our body organs, that is, the perception of beings at three different levels, such as feelings, mind and heart.

The point we want to emphasize here is that Al-Ghazali was able to determine the sequence of embryological development stages of human organs in accordance with today's modern embryology data, while drawing such a table of knowledge theory. We covered this matter earlier.[42] Let's try to explain this point briefly.

Whether Al-Ghazali brought out the stages of embryological development logically from a theory of knowledge as explained earlier, or on the contrary, knowing the embryological stages first, he established the theory of knowledge as its logical consequence (although the first hypothesis seems more correct to us), is not important. In any case, it is a scientific determination of the embryological development of humans.

---

42. M. Bayrakdar, "Parallelism between the Acquisition of Knowledge and the Embryological Development of the Organs of Knowledge According to Imam al-Ghazali", *National Education and Culture*, Year 5, Issue 20, March, 1983, pp. 15–20.

Sensory organs are in the first stage, and the first of these is the skin. According to modern embryology, the first layer to form is the ectoderm. After that, it is the outer skin and other sensory organs. A large part of the eye, especially the retina and lens, is made up of the ectoderm.[43]

Al-Ghazali first said in his book *The Alchemy of Happiness* (*Kimya-e-Saadet*) that the eye consisted of ten layers,[44] while later in the same book at another other place he said that the eye consisted of seven layers.[45] The modern view admits that the eye consists of seven layers. That is why Al-Ghazali accepted the first knowledge as the functions of these organs.

The human brain is made up of the endoderm in the second stage of embryological development. More precisely, it consists of the first endoderm cells of the ectoderm. That is why Al-Ghazali regards secondary knowledge, or mental knowledge, as the functions of the brain. According to Al-Ghazali, the brain activates to produce knowledge in order to fully realize its job of thinking starts at the age of seven.

According to Al-Ghazali, the heart is formed at the last stage. Modern embryology also says that the heart is formed in the last phase, the mesoderm stage. More precisely, the heart consists of the lateral mesoderm, which is the advanced development of the mesoderm.[46] As can be seen, there is a correspondence between Al-Ghazali's views and modern views.

The embryological development of humans has occupied scientists since ancient times. Aristotle and especially Galen

---

43. Black's Medical Dictionary, p. 344; Şeref Yazgan, General Embryology Lecture Notes, p. 35.
44. Al-Ghazali, *Kimya-e-Saadet* (*The Alchemy of Happiness*), Tehran, Vol. II, p. 789.
45. Ibid., p. 945.
46. Şeref Yazgan, p. 41; Henry Gras, Anatomy of the Human Body, 29th edition, Philadelphia, 1973, p. 27.

had said a lot about this; but they had no opinions that continue to be held scientifically correct until today. For example, Galen considered the heart to be the most important organ of the human being and so considered it to be the first organ that formed in humans. Even the great medical scholar, Ibn Sina, perhaps under the influence of Galen, had accepted that heart was the first organ to be formed in the human body. Considering the lack of scientific anatomical research at that time, we can consider the errors of Ibn Sina and others as reasonable. But we should appreciate the fact that someone like Al-Ghazali, who was not a doctor like them and nor did he grow up in a similar environment as theirs. His environment was not very suitable for advanced research. Yet he pointed to some very modern views on this issue.

To illustrate all of this, let's study the following scheme:

Sequence No.	Knowledge Phase	Embryological Phase
1.	Sensations and Needs (Sensory knowledge)	Ectoderm: Most of sensory organs
2.	Permissible (Mental knowledge)	Endoderm: Brain and nerves
3.	Knowledge and Observations (Heart and discovered knowledge)	Mesoderm: Heart and some other organs

The Sufi Whirling or Sema Ceremony and the Structure of the Universe and the Atom

Forms of worship and zikr (an Islamic prayer where a phrase or expression of praise is repeated continually) such as sema ceremony (whirling of dervishes) and dance predate Mevlana Rumi in the history of Sufism. However, sema ceremony that was shaped by Mevlana Rumi himself, also carries special meanings that it expresses symbolically. Let's briefly dwell on these meanings. We have covered this issue in a few articles before.[47] The Mevlevi sema ceremony symbolizes creation and the structure of the whole universe before everything. In order to understand these symbols, it is necessary to visualize and bring the Mevlevi sema before our eyes.

1. Sema Ceremony, the First Creation and the Last Creation

First of all, sema ceremony symbolizes the first and last creation– the creation of the universe and the human beings together with the resurrection. The black colour of the robes of the dervishes entering the place where they perform sema represents the nothingness and darkness. In order to begin the sema ceremony, the dervishes first sit on the ground, then throw their robes off and stand up in their white clothes. All this represents the creation of being and expresses that everything is the external manifestation of the knowledge of Allah. Since there is no difference between the first creation and the resurrection, the black robes also represent the grave. The black robes being thrown off and the standing up of the dervish in the white dress represent the act of rising from the grave and the Day of Judgement. These are the metaphysical meaning of the sema ceremony.

2. Sema Ceremony, the Structure of the Universe and the Atom

Second, the sema ceremony symbolizes the structure of both the universe and the atom together. For Sufis, there is no

---
47. M. Bayrakdar, "Mawlana's View on the Divisibility of Atoms", *Muslimedia*, June 1984.

difference between the structure of the whole universe and the structure of a single atom. The sheikh who conducts the sema ceremony and is in the middle of the dervishes also represents the sun in the middle of the solar system as well as the atomic nucleus at the centre of the atom. Dervishes represent both planets orbiting the sun and electrons around atomic nuclei, at the same time. The whirling dervishes around the sheikh, who is also in motion, represent the universe and atoms being in constant motion together as well as separate entities.

Some of the Mevlevi writers have earlier pointed out that sema represents the solar system. According to this, the centre of our solar system is the sun represented by the sheikh. Mevlana Rumi and Mevlevi dervishes pointed out that the sun was the centre of the solar system, even though it contradicted traditional belief held at that time. As it is known, Aristotle and Ptolemy and almost all scholars before Mavlana Rumi considered the earth as the centre, excluding some Muslim scholars such as Al-Sijzi.

However, it has not been pointed out by the previous authors that the sema ceremony also symbolizes the structure of the atom. Our attention to this point arises from our knowledge of the structure of the atom today but never goes ahead of just establishing a connection. Indeed, Mevlana Rumi himself was a sign of this. This may not have caught the attention of the old authors. Therefore, the subject may not have been covered earlier.

> In one of his poems we mentioned earlier, Mevlana Rumi said:
>
> *If you cut an atom,*
>
> *A sun in the middle*
>
> *And around the sun too*
>
> *You find planets that rotate continuously.*

Here, Mevlana Rumi quite clearly compares the internal structure of an atom to the solar system. He points to the nucleus of the atom and the particles spinning around it that we today call electrons.

On the other hand, there is a historical indication that Mevlana Rumi took the structure of the atom as an example, not the solar system, while shaping his unique sky. El-Eflaki, one of the famous Mevlevi writers, briefly states the following while telling the story of the Mevlevi sema ceremony in his work *Menaqibu'l-Arifin*:

> One day, when Mevlana was passing through the Konya bazaar, he paused when he heard the sound of gold particles (atoms) groaning from being beaten under the hammer in the shop of the jeweller Selahaddin (Salah al-Din Zarkub), who would later become his friend. After listening and thinking thoroughly, he suddenly started to do sema in the middle of the street. This was the beginning of the Mevlevi sema.

We understand from this that Mevlana Rumi himself first symbolized the structure of the atom while doing his sema and took its structure as an example to his formation of Mevlevi sema ceremony.

Conclusion

When Sufism is considered as a whole and as it developed in history, it appears to be a true form of religious life as well as a discipline that contributes to politics, economics, science and art. As it happened in the past too, for some reason or the other, people who favour Sufism and who are against it, both are present.

It would be appropriate to remind here that no branch of knowledge or science has descended from the sky in a wicker basket. All of them have been compiled by human beings over time and in accordance with the needs of human beings. Every science has emerged as a result of a necessity. We cannot say that any science is good or bad in itself; only the kindness or malice of the one who engages in the particular field of sciences can be a matter of consideration in this regard. In this context, there can be good as well as bad ones also among the Sufis who deal with Sufism. Just as there are good as well as bad jurisprudents who deal with Islamic jurisprudence, which is considered as one of the most Islamic and religious sciences or branch of knowledge, there are good and bad Sufis, too. Consequently, everything begins and ends with the human being. If a sheikh or a mystic learns the sciences of the world and religion, humans and society, and educates himself well, Sufism is good and useful. This is valid for all the sciences and the scientists. Just as half a doctor is a danger to people's life, half a sheikh poses danger to one's faith.

Conclusion

Sufis have always supported the good in political life, have been interested in domestic politics, have been able to take a stand against unfair and unjust practices to which the official Muslim clergy have surrendered, and have been able to wage war for freedom against external enemies and colonialists. The history of Sufism is full of such examples. Most of the wars of independence in North Africa and the Indian-Pakistani Peninsula were fought under the guidance of Sufis. Many a time, Sufis revitalized economic and social life, established social assistance institutions, did not eat their food and fed others with that, and gave their clothes to the needy. Sufis also raised many artists and crafts persons. The best calligraphers and the best musicians produced by the Islamic world are also Sufis. The music pieces that we still listen to with pleasure are the works of Sufis. The best poets, many of whom are admired by the entire world today, are Sufis. As we tried to explain in the framework of this book, there were also Sufi scientists and they contributed to the development of science. It is possible to give countless examples of all these dimensions of Sufism. But we want to finish our work without counting them all and with these lines:

From the beginning until the end of the twentieth century, the most heroic, most famous and most unforgettable men of military, political and intellectual excellence, no matter what part of the Islamic world, have always been Sufis or people who engaged themselves with this branch of knowledge and science at some point of their lives. From Abu Darr al-Ghifari to Al-Ghazali; from Hasan al-Basri to Emir Abdelkader to Sudanese Mahdi and Sheikh Shamil; from Saadi Shirazi, from Mevlana Rumi and Muhyiddin Ibn Arabi to Mehmet Tahir of Bursa; from Bayazid Bastami to Mohammad Iqbal and Hassan al-Banna; from Ibn Taymiyyah to the Physics Nobel Prize winner Abdus Salam . . .

BIBLIOGRAPHY

Al-Ghazali, *Al-Munqidh min al-dalal*. 2nd edition (Farid Jabr publication, Beirut, 1969).

Al-Ghazali, *Al-Risatu'l-Leddunya*. 2nd edition. Translated by A. Şener and Ş. Topaloğlu (Istanbul, 1973).

Al-Ghazali. *Ihya' Ulum al-Din* (Aleppo publication, Cairo, 1302).

Al-Ghazali, *Kimya-e-Saadet* (*The Alchemy of Happiness*) (Tehran, 1318).

Al-Ghazali. *Mishkat al-Anwar* (Cairo, 1353).

Al-Ghazali. *Mustafa Fi Usul ud-din* (Cairo, 1356).

Al-Hallaj, Mansur. *Kitab al-Tawasin* (L. Massignon, Paris, 1913).

Al-Hujwiri, Ali. *Kashf al-Mahjub*. Translated by R.A. Nicholson (London, 1911).

Al-Iraqi, *Kitabu'l-Ilmi'l-Muqtasab fi Zira'ati'z-Zahab*. English translation by E.J. Holyard (Paris, 1923).

Al-Qaysari, Dawud. *Matla' Khususi'l-Kelim fi Ma'ani Fusus al-Hikam* (Bombay, 1881).

Al-Qaysari, Dawud. *Tahqiqu Mâ'i'l-Hayat ve Kashfu Esrâri'z-Zulumât*. Translated by M. Bayrakdar, *Dawud from Kayseri* (Ministry of Culture and Tourism Publications, Ankara, 1988).

Al-Qunawi, Sadr al-Din. *Fourty Hadith*. Turkish translation by A. Akçiçek (Istanbul, 1970).

Al-Qunawi, Sadr al-Din. *al-Hadis"l-Erba'in*. Translated by A. Akçiçek (Istanbul, 1970).

Bibliography

Al-Qurtubi. *Tafsir*. vol. 18 (Cairo, 1949).

As-Sadiq, Ja'far. *Kitab Risala Ja'far al-Sadiq fi Ilm al-Sana'a Wal-Hajar al-Muqarram*. German translation by J. Ruska (Heidelberg, 1924).

Bayrakdar, M. "Being and Existential Diversification in Ibn Arabi". *Ankara University, Journal of the Faculty of Theology*. vol. XXV, 1981.

Bayrakdar, M. "Cosmological Relativity of Ibn Arabi". *Islamic Culture*. vol. 58, no. 3, 1984.

Bayrakdar, M."Learning about the World and Post-Death Events by Dreaming According to İbrahim Hakkı Erzurumi". *National Education and Culture*. Issue 25, 1984.

Bayrakdar, M. "Mawlana's View on the Divisibility of Atoms". *Muslimedia*, June 1984.

Bayrakdar, M. "Parallelism between the Acquisition of Knowledge and the Embryological Development of the Organs of Knowledge According to Imam al-Ghazali". *National Education and Culture*. Year 5, Issue 20, March 1983.

Bayrakdar, M., "Relativity and Similarities According to al-Kindi and Einstein". *Science and Technology*. issue 153, 1980,

Berthelot, M. *La chimie au moyen âge*. 3 volumes (Paris, 1893).

Black's Medical Dictionary. 13th edition (London, 1974).

Burnet J. *Early Greek Philosophy*. Reprint (London, 1971).

Bursevi, I. H.*Kenz-i Mahfi. Hidden Secrets*. Translated by Abdülkadir Akçiçek (Kitsan Publications, Istanbul, 1997).

Cicero. *On the Nature of the Gods* (London, 1941).

Corbin, H. *L'Imagination Créatrice dans le soufisme d'Ibn' Arabî*. 2nd edition (Paris, 1976).

Dagognet F. *Philosophie biologique* (Paris, 1955).

Edwards, P. "Panpsychism". *The Encyclopedia of Philosophy*. vol. 6 (New York, London, 1967).

Eralp, T.N. *The Concept of Weapons in Turkish Society throughout History and Weapons Used in the Ottoman Empire* (TTK Pub., Ankara, 1993).

El-Eflaki, Shemsud-Din Ahmed, *Menqibu'l-Arifin*. Translated by J.W. Redhouse (Quest Books, U.S., 1976)

Erzurumi, İbrahim Hakkı. *Marifetname* (Istanbul, 1881).

Fechner, G.T. *Religion of a Scientist*. English translation by W. Lowrie (New York, 1946).

Feyerabend, P. K. *Against Method: Outline of an Anarchist Theory of Knowledge* (London, 1975).

Freud, S. *Le rêve et son interprétation*. French translation by H. Legros, Paris, 1925.

Guthier W.K.C. *A History of Greek Philosophy*. vol. I (Cambridge, 1962).

Holmyard E.J. *Works of Geber*. Translated by Robert Russell, 1678. Reprint. (London–Toronto, 1928).

Holmyard, E.J. *Makers of Chemistry* (Oxford, 1931).

Ibn al-Farid. *Diwan* (Cairo, undated).

Ibn Arabi. *Al-Futuhat Al-Makkiyah* (*The Meccan Revelations*). 4 volumes (Cairo, 1329).

Ibn Arabi, *Fusus al-Hikam*. Translated by M.N. Gençosman, *The Bezels of Wisdom* (Ministry of Education, Ankara, 1952)

Ibn Battuta. *Rihla*. French translation by Defrémery et B. R. Sanguinetti. vol. I (Paris, 1814).

Jabir Ibn Hayyan. *Traité de la Miséricorde*. French translation by M. Berthelot, *La chimie au moyen âge*. vol. III (Paris, 1893).

Jurjani, Ibn Sina ve.*Sîretü'ş-Şeyhi'r-Râîs*. English translation by W.E. Gohlman, *The Life of Ibn Sina* (Albany, New York, 1974).

Khan, M.M. trans. *Sahih al-Bukhari*. vol. II (Ankara, 1976).

Mevlana Rumi. *Diwan* (Tehran, 1336).

Mevlana Rumi. *Fihi Ma Fihi*. English translation by A.J. Arberry (London, 1961).

Mevlana Rumi. *Masnavi*. English translation and commentary by R.A. Nicholson (Luzac, London, 1925–1937).

Mevlana Rumi. *Rubaiyat*. French translation by A. H. Çelebi (Paris, 1946).

Palacios, A.M. *Huellas del Islam* (Madrid, 1941).

Saadi, Sheikh. *The Gulistân*. English translation by J.P. Platts. 2nd ed. (London, 1887).

Schopenhauer, A. *On the Will in Nature*. English translation by K. Hillebrand (London, 1889).

Shabestari, Mahmoud. *Gulshan-i Raz*. English translation by E.H. Whinfield. Reprint (Lahore, 1978).

Yazgan, Şeref. *General Embryology Lecture Notes*.

Zukav, G. *The Dancing Wu Li Masters* (London, 1979).

INDEX

Al-Munqidh min al-dalal 74
Abdelkader, Emir 83
Against Method 9, 86
ahl-e-kashf 46
Akshemseddin 34, 35
Al-Banna, Hassan 83
Al-Basri, Hasan 83, 96
Al-Biruni 3
Al-Bitruji xii
alchemists 54, 55
alchemy 23, 24, 25, 26, 29
Alchemy of Happiness 77, 84
Al-Farabi 66
Al-Farid, Ibn 59, 86
Al-Ghazali 12, 14, 31, 32, 59, 71, 72, 74, 75, 76, 78, 83
Al-Ghifari, Abu Darr 83
Al-Haytham 3
Al-Iksir 55
Al-Iraki 55
Al-Khalwati, Shaheen 29
Al-Khazini 3
Al-Kindi xi, 67
Almagest 25
Al-Maghribi, Abu Osman 49
Al-Misri, Dhul-Nun xv, 29
Al-Qaysari, Dawud 59, 67, 70, 71, 84
Al-Qunawi, Sadr al-Din 34, 68, 84
Al-Qurtubi 63, 64, 85
Al-Razi, Abu Bakr xiii, 2, 24, 66
Al-Razi, Abu Bakr Zakariya 28
Al-Risatu'l-Leddunya 72, 84
Al-Sadiq, Ja'far 24, 25, 86
Al-Shirazi, Qutb al-Din 34
Al-Sijzi 80
Al-Sufi, Abd-al Rahman 30, 31
Al-Tusi, Nasir al-Din 34
Al-Tusi, Sheikh Abul Qasim Gurgani 49
Al-Zamakhshari 47
ammonium cyanate 50
Anaxagoras xi, xii
Anaxagoras and the Birth of Scientific Method xi
animal life 45, 46
animal person 17

Index

animal soul 72
animism 53
An-Nablusi 29
Arabi, Muhyiddin Ibn 45, 83
Archimedes 3, 4
Archimedes' Principle 3
Argelander 31
Aristotelian–Newtonian tradition 50
Aristotle 25, 55, 66, 77, 80
As-Simavi, Abul Qasim Muhammed bin Ahmed 55
astrology 23, 24
astronomer Sufis 30
astronomy x, xi, xii, xiii, 23, 24, 25, 30, 32, 33, 34, 63,
astrophysics 50
atomism 9, 57
atoms 6, 48, 50, 57, 60, 79, 80, 85
August Kekulé, Friedrich 13, 50
ayn-ul-yaqeen 18

Babylon 54
Babylonians x, xiii
Bacon, Francis xi
Baghdad xii
Barkhiya, Asif ibn 69
Barzakh Realm 18
Bastami, Bayazid 83

Bell 6
Bergson, Henri 10, 11
Berzelius 51
beta distortion (beta detail) 60, 61
Beyzavi 47
Bilqis 69
biology 50
Book of Fixed Stars 30
Bouligand, Georges 12
Brouwer 12

Calder, Ritchie xi
Cardano xi
Cartan, Elie 12
Cartesian philosophy 8
Chardin, P. Teilhard de 52
Chemistry 2, 23, 24, 25, 26, 28, 29, 46, 50, 53, 56
Chinese x
Christianity 1
cleansing of the self 20, 21
Comte, August 7
conquest 20, 21, 35
Contradiction 2
Copernican Revolution, The xi, 9
Copernicus xi
Corbin, Henry 70,
cosmological energetism 71
Crookes, Sir William 5

Dalton 6
Damascus Gate of Baghdad xiii, 2
dark room (camera obscura) 3, 6
Darwin 8
Demirtaş, Şemseddin Muhammed 29
Descartes 10
Die Energie 71
discovered knowledge 76, 78
discovery 4, 7, 14, 20, 22, 35, 45, 46, 51
Divine Light of Mohammad 70
Doctor of the Bodies 35
Doctor of the Souls 35
Dream 12, 13, 14, 18s, 36, 54, 56s, 57s,

Ectoderm 77, 78
Eddington, Arthur 65
Edison 4, 5
Eye of the Heart 24, 71, 72, 73, 75, 76
Egypt 29, 54
Egyptians xiii
Einstein, A. 66
electron 60, 61
El-Eflaki 81

Elements of Geometry xii, 25
emotional knowledge 75
Endoderm 77, 78
Enlightenment 1, 3
epistemology 9
Erzurumi, İbrahim Hakkı 13, 32, 33
Euclid xii, 25
existence (permanence) 58
extinction (annihilation) 58

Feshner, G.T. 52
Feyerabend, Paul K. 9
Feynman diagrams 61
Fihi Ma Fihi 48
First Intelligence (see Divine Light of Mohammad) 70
First Matter (see Prima Materia) 70
Fracastorius, Girolamo 35
Freud, S. 12

Galen 77, 78
Gershenson, Daniel E. xi
Goethe 52
Greece 57
Greenberg, Daniel xi

Haji Bayram Veli 35
haqq-ul-yaqeen 18

Hayyan, Jabir ibn
heart 13, 15, 18, 19, 20, 21, 24, 40. 60, 71, 72, 73, 75, 76, 77, 78
Hegel 11
Helmholtz 71
Hey'etü', l-Islam 33
Heyting, A. 12
Hubble, E. 65
human life 45
Husserl, Edmund 10
hylozoism 51, 53, 54

Ihya' Ulum al-Din 12, 72
ilm-ul-yaqeen 18
Imamia sect 25
inspiration 5, 19, 20, 21, 22, 47, 59, 60
intuition 10, 11, 14, 15, 16, 21, 36, 45, 46, 59, 60, 68
intuitionism 11
Iqbal, Mohammad 83
Islamic scientific trdition 1
İzniki, Ali Bey 24

Jansky, K.G. 6
Jayib Board 33

Kant 10, 66
Khall-e Mushkilat 35
Khalwati sect 29

Khidr 67, 69
Kitabu'l-Aca'ib 29
Kuhn, Thomas S. x

Lavoisier 51
law of buoyancy 3, 4
Law of Gravity 4
Le rêve et son interprétation 12
Lemaitre, Abbe 65
Lenin 71
Les aspects intuitifs de la Mathématique 12
Levi b.en Gerson xi
Lisan al-Arab 63
Lodge, Sir Oliver 6

Mackenzie, Sir James 6
Madina Mosque 49
Mahdi, Sudanese 83
Maidat ul-Hayat 35
manifestation 19, 20, 21, 20, 23, 48, 49, 52, 53, 60, 61, 79
Maraga Madrasa 34
Marifetname 13, 32, 33
Maxwell 5
medicine 24, 34, 35, 73
Menaqibu'l-Arifin 81
Menâzil-i Kamer 33
Mendel xiii

Mendel Law xiii
mental knowledge 75, 76, 77, 78
Mesoderm 77, 78
metaphysics 10, 14, 24
Mevlevi sema ceremony 79, 81
Middle East 57
Miletus school 53
Milky Way 6
modern science ix, x, 21, 22, 49, 50, 57, 72
modernity x
Muslims xi, 23, 62

Nafs al-Ammara 16, 17
Nafs al-Kamil 17, 19
Nafs al-Lawwama 16, 17
Nafs al-Marziyyah 17, 19
Nafs al-Mulhamah 16, 18
Nafs al-Mutma'inna 16, 18
Nafs al-Raziyyah 17, 19
needs 13, 76, 78, 82
neutrino 61
neutrons 56
New Age xi
New Scientist 13
Newton 4, 50
North Africa 29, 83

observations xiii, 3, 15, 30, 51, 76, 78

Organic Knowledge Theory 74
Ostwald, Wilhelm 71

panbioism 44, 46, 49, 50, 51, 52, 53, 54
panpsychism 51, 52, 53, 54
passing of space 66, 67
passing of time 66, 67
Pasteur, Louis 35
people of Ur xi
permissible 10, 75, 76, 78
phenomenology 10, 11
philosophical animism 53
philosophy xiii, 8, 9, 10, 11, 15, 21, 32, 54, 66
philosophy of science 8
photon 60, 61
physics 14, 24, 34, 46, 50, 53, 60, 66, 83
Plato 25
Platonism 29
positivism xi, xiv, 1, 2, 3, 11, 14
Prima Materia 70
Prophet Mohammad 49, 70
Prophet Solomon 49, 69
proton 56, 57, 60, 61
psychophysics xi
Ptolemy 25, 63, 80
Ptolemy astronomy 63
pure reason 10

Index

Pythagoras x
Pythagoras Theorem ix
Pythagoreanism 51

quantum 9, 50, 61
quantum mechanics 50
quantum-relativity theory 61

real dreams 12
Realm of Magnificence 18
Realm of the Angels 18
Realm of the Divine 19
Realm of the Unseen 19, 20
re-creation 58, 59, 60, 61
Reform 1
relativity 50, 61, 66, 67
Renaissance xi, 1
revelation 20, 21, 46,
Risalat an-Nuriya 35
Röntgen 5, 6
Röntgen rays 6
Rubbü'l-Müceyyeb 33
Ruknu Ahbar 29
Rumi, Mevlana Rumi 44, 48, 52, 58, 59, 79, 80, 81, 83
Ruşeni, Dede Ömer 29
Ruska, Julius 25
Rutherford xv

Salam, Abdus 83
sameness 2

Schatzman, Morton 13
Schiller, F.C.S. 52
Schopenhauer, A. 52
sema ceremony 78, 79, 80, 81
sensations 76, 78
seven earths 63, 64
seven heavens 46, 63, 64
Shamil, Sheikh 83
Sharh Kulliyat'l-Qanun 34
Shemseddin Mehmed bin Hamza 34
Shifai, Omer 24
Shirazi, Saadi 59, 83,
Sikah 29
Sina, Ibn 21, 34, 78,
Sitter, Willem de 65
Socrates 25
soul 13, 15, 16, 17, 18, 20, 21, 36, 44, 45, 46, 47, 48, 49, 51, 52, 53, 70
Spiritual Eye (see Third Eye) 72
Spiritual Heart (see Third Eye)
State of Testimony 20
Stoicism 51
Stoics 50
subatomic 50
subatomic dance 51
subatomic particles 50, 57, 60, 61,

Sufis xii, 14, 17, 22, 23, 24, 25, 34, 36, 37, 44, 45, 46, 47, 48, 49, 51, 52, 54, 57, 58, 59, 60, 61, 62, 63, 64, 66, 67, 69, 70, 71, 72, 73, 83,

Sufism viii, ix, x, xiii, 13, 14, 15, 16, 21, 25, 29, 32, 34, 44, 79, 82, 83

Tahir, Mehmet of Bursa 83
Tajul Arus 63
Taymiyyah, Ibn 83
the absence of the third state 2
The Canon of Medicine 34
The Fourth State of Matter 5
The Incoherence of the Philosophers 32
theology 15
Third Eye 72
Til al-Harmel xii
Tractatus de Planets 32
true soul 72

Uluğ Bey 30
Universal Mind (see Universal Soul) 51
Universal Soul (see Divine Light of Muohammad) 51, 70,
urea 50

Waddington, C.H. 52
Wahadat al-Wujud 14
Wards of the Lord xii
Western mind xi
Western race xi
Westerners x, ix, 25
Wisdom 18, 20, 22, 47, 62,
Wöhler, Friedrich 50

X-rays 5, 6

Yazid, Khalid ibn 25
Yunus, Ibn 30

Zarkub, Salah al-Din 81
Zeno 51

Translator's Note

There has been a striking perseverance in every age of history of humankind to align the curiosity of both the physical and the spiritual world. Unfortunately these waves of science and spirituality have hardly been able to blend into each other in order to reveal its own beauty and miracle. Human fallibility is to blame for the extreme approach in life. Sufism proves to display a balanced life of both religious and thinking person.

This book about Sufism and Modern Science sheds light on the relationship between Science and Sufism in Islamic history and philosophy. Sufism is essentially a discipline of psychology and morality. It cleanses the human mind and heart of empty and redundant thoughts. The cleansed and purged mind and heart enables the person to attain truth and consciousness in what he or she perceives and does. The culmination of both the ideas gives people the quality of creativity. Al-Ghazali, Mevlana Rumi, Hasan al-Basri, Akshemseddin and Ahmed Süreyya Emin Bey are just some of the names in the long list of Sufis who contributed to the field of science and philosophy.

From the process of converting one element into another to the idea of overcoming time and space, Sufis have silently worked on and contributed to several theories and theorems. Although this was not their main duty, they were pioneers in the positive sciences. Some Sufis used such symbolic expressions which could be related by the terms given by scientists, developed centuries later. From this, it is possible to sense the depth of the scientific foresight of the Sufis who also helped untangle the obstructed horizons of positive sciences. This book enlightens the people of the lost history of science which was immensely enriched by the Sufis in different periods of time.

Dr Mohsin Ali